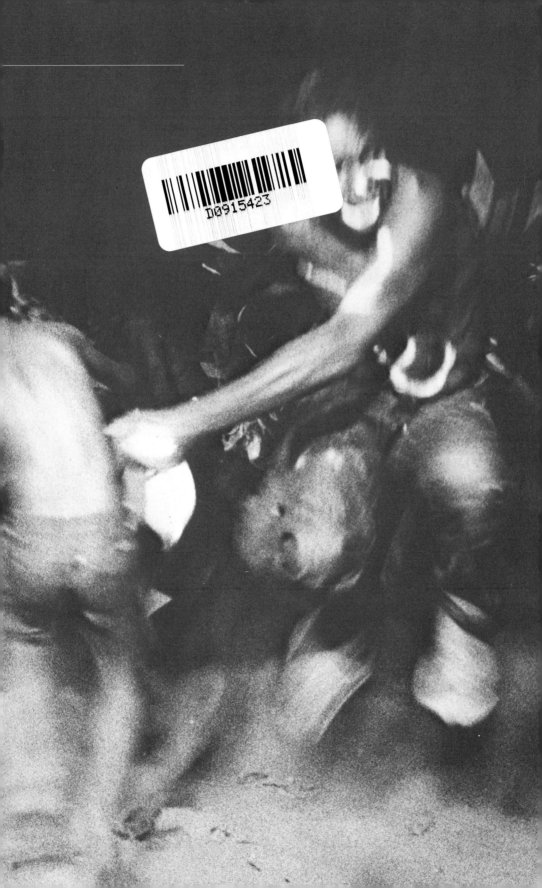

The new frontier

The new frontier

Australia's rising northwest

Jeff Carter

ANGUS AND ROBERTSON

First published in 1971 by

ANGUS & ROBERTSON LTD

221 George Street, Sydney
107 Elizabeth Street, Melbourne
89 Anson Road, Singapore
54 Bartholomew Close, London

National Library of
Australia card number and
ISBN 0 207 12146 X

PRINTED IN HONG KONG

Contents

Photographs

Maps

All photographs are by Jeff Carter,
except where otherwise acknowledged

Exploration

The first foreigners to set foot on the coast of northwest Australia may have been Chinese navigators, in the early 1400s. Chinese relics were dug up on the present site of Darwin in 1879. One, a small image of *Shou-Lac,* the Chinese god of long life, is in the Technological Museum, Sydney. A scholar claims to have discovered Chinese writings that mention the discovery of Australia round 560 B.C. some 2,000 years before the first Europeans arrived.

Matthew Flinders encountered Macassan fishermen off the coast of Arnhem Land in 1803. Recent archaeological discoveries indicate Malayan seafarers established camps on the northwest mainland long before the arrival of Europeans. The Macassans, from the Celebes Islands, were chiefly interested in trepang, an edible sea slug ("beche-de-mer"), very popular in China. They came in wooden praus of 10 to 25 tons. The trepang was boiled down and dried at settlements along the coast from Arnhem Land to the Kimberleys.

The Malayans came for turtles, dugong and pearl shell. Usually, the visitors got on well with the Aborigines, who worked with them during the fishing season. There was some trading between the seafarers and the Aborigines. Occasional clashes took place, sometimes incited by drink, which the traders brought with them. There were also squabbles over women. Some Aborigines sailed to the islands north of Australia with the traders, and returned home with them the following season.

All of the early European navigators exploring the northwest coast met Macassan praus or found signs of the trepang fishery. Matthew Flinders wrote of 60 praus in one area, with 1,000 men on board. Other estimates put the total number of regular Malayan and Macassan visitors to the northwest at 3,000.

Although they weren't the first discoverers, Europeans suspected the existence of an Australian land mass long before they set eyes on it. The map of the known world made by Ptolemy of Alexandria in 150 A.D. showed *Terra Incognita* amid the unchartered oceans east of Africa and south of Asia. Marco Polo suggested the existence of a large continent south of Java in the 13th century.

No one knows for sure the identity of the first European to reach Australia's

1

western shores. The *Picturesque Atlas of Australasia,* published in 1886, states that in 1527 "the Portuguese Menezes discovered the west Australian shores . . . " (This was probably Don Jorge de Menezes, who sailed along the northern coast of New Guinea in 1526.)

The first documented landing didn't take place until 1616, but it is almost certain that some Portuguese navigators discovered Australia's west coast almost a century earlier. An atlas published in Antwerp in 1593 depicts a kangaroo-like animal, with twin joeys in its pouch.

After 1611, Dutch ships bound for the East Indies avoided the doldrums of the central Indian Ocean by sailing east from the Cape of Good Hope for almost 4,000 miles, before heading north for Batavia. Navigation was far from an exact science in those days, so inevitably some Dutch ships overshot their turning point and came to Australia's western shores.

One of them, the *Eendracht,* under Captain Dirck Hartog, sailed too far east, and made a landfall on an island at Shark Bay, near the present port of Carnarvon. This was in 1616. The island was named Dirck Hartog Island and the discoverers left a tin plate on a post to mark their landing.

In 1618, another Dutchman, Lenaert Jacobsz, landed his ship *Mauritius* at Exmouth Gulf. Like Hartog, he was en route for the Spice Islands of the East Indies and wasted little time exploring the area. A chart made by Captain Gerrit Frederikszoon de Witt in 1628 shows that his ship *Vyanen* ran briefly aground in that year somewhere near what is now Port Hedland.

One of the first Englishmen to touch the northwest coast was Captain John Brook in the *Tryal.* He made landfall at Point Cloats in May, 1622, and was wrecked several weeks later. Ninety-two people lost their lives and considerable treasure went to the bottom on what is now called Tryal Rocks north of Barrow Island. Brooke and forty or more survivors eventually reached Batavia in two small boats.

The next Dutch visitors to Western Australia struck real tragedy on 4th June, 1629. Captain Francois Pelsaert's ship *Batavia* was wrecked on one of the Abrolhos islands, some 40 miles off shore from present-day Geraldton. Seventy lives were lost and 220 frightened passengers were landed on two adjoining islands. There was little water salvaged and none on the islands. In a ship's boat, Pelsaert and some of his men sailed to the mainland in search of water. They found none until they had struggled to North West Cape, a distance of about 400 miles. Here they found a few gallons, scarcely enough for their own needs.

So they sailed on for 1,800 miles to Batavia, where they arrived on 7th July, 1629.

A few days later, Pelsaert sailed in the *Sardam* to rescue survivors from his wrecked *Batavia.* Reaching the island, he found some of his crew had murdered 125 of the passengers. The 34 mutineers were clapped in chains, and all but two of them were summarily executed on Seal Island. The two reprieved mutineers were abandoned on the mainland, Pelsaert's idea being "That this punishment may ultimately rebound to the services of the (East India) Company, and that the two delinquents may come off with their lives, so as to be able to give trustworthy information about these parts". Nothing was ever heard of these two castaways.

Pelsaert salvaged eight of the nine treasure chests off the wrecked *Batavia.* Then he departed with the survivors from his ill-fated ship. In 1644, Abel Janszoon Tasman was ordered to search for the other chest, which contained "eight thousand rix dollars"——but failed to do so. Tasman made a voyage from Batavia to Cape York, and then westward round the northwest coast of Australia to the Ashburton River, near North West Cape. He was the first European to chart the coastline of what is now Australia's "New Frontier".

The pirate ship *Cygnet* under Captain Read, with William Dampier on board, was the next English ship on the northwest coast. The *Cygnet* was beached on Cape Leveque, on the northwest corner of King Sound, on 4th January, 1688. Cleaning operations and some minor repairs were carried out while casks of fresh water were loaded.

Crowds of Aborigines watched proceedings, but couldn't be induced to help with the work. Dampier wrote: *But all the signs we could make were to no purpose; for they stood there like statues, staring at one another, and grinning like so many monkeys. These poor creatures seemed not accustomed to carry burdens. The inhabitants of this Country are the miserablest in the world. The Hodmadods of Monomatapa, though a nasty people, yet for wealth are gentlemen to these who have no houses and skin garments, sheep, poultry, and fruits of the earth, as the Hodmadods have: and setting aside their human shape, they differ but little from brutes. They are tall, straight bodied and thin, with small long limbs. They have great heads, round foreheads and great brows. Their eyelids are always half closed, to keep the flies out of their eyes: they being so troublesome here, that no fanning will keep them from coming to one's face; and without the assistance of both hands to keep them off, they will creep into one's nostrils; and mouth too, if the lips are not shut very close. So that from their infancy being thus annoyed with these insects, they do never open their eyes, as other people: and therefore they cannot see far . . . Their only food is a small sort of fish, which they get by making wares (traps) of stone, across little coves, or branches of the sea: every tide bringing in the small fish, and there leaving them a prey for these people who constantly attend there, to search for them at low water . . . When they have eaten, they lye down till the next low water . . . the earth affords them no food at all. There is neither herb, root, pulse nor any sort of grain, for them to eat, that we saw: not any sort of bird, or beast that they can catch, having no instruments wherewithal to do so . . .*

Although his report on northwest Australia was very unfavourable, Dampier took home to England an optimistic tale of riches to be won by plundering Dutch ships trading in the Spice Islands. He was given command of a 290-ton, 12-gun naval ship *Roebuck.*

In this he reached the Abrolhos on 1st August, 1699. Then he sailed north for several days, landing on the mainland at Shark Bay on 5th August. He explored this area for a week, encountering wallabies on Dirck Hartog Island. Of these he wrote: *The Land Animals that we saw here were only a Sort of Raccoons, different from those of the West Indies, chiefly as to their Legs; for these have very short Fore-legs; but go jumping upon them as the others do and like them are very good Meat.* (Dampier was describing the banded hare-wallaby — *Lagostrophus fasciatus*.)

Dampier was not the first European to describe a member of the kangaroo family, however. Pelsaert's journal mentions the tammar wallaby (*Wallabia eugenii*), following his shipwreck in the Abrolhos in 1629.

After Dampier, the next Englishman to visit Australia's northwestern shores was Captain Phillip Parker King, in 1818. Sailing from Sydney in the 84-ton cutter *Mermaid*, he crossed the Great Australian Bight to King George Sound (now Albany). After taking on wood and water, he sailed round the southwestern corner of the continent and then north round North West Cape (site of the present American radio base). Off Nickol Bay, where Roebourne now stands, King sighted and named Pyramid Hill, about 30 miles inland. King also named Roebuck Bay, the present site of Broome, after Dampier's ship.

In 1819, King surveyed the north coast of Arnhem Land and the west Kimberley coast. His most detailed investigations were conducted southwesterward from Cape Londonderry to Cape Voltaire. His ship explored Napier Broome Bay, Vansittart Bay and Admiralty Gulf.

King found ample evidence of Malay landings along the coast and signs of a well-established trepang fishery.

The first major attempt at exploration of the northwest mainland was attempted by Captain George Grey in 1837. Arriving directly from England, with no previous experience of Australia, Grey had the rather grandiose and impractical plan to travel overland to the settlement at Perth, established in 1829.

On 3rd December, 1837, Grey went ashore with five companions on Hanover Bay, just south of the entrance of the Prince Regent River. It turned out to be an inauspicious occasion.

Grey wrote: *We soon gained the edge of a sandy beach, on which I sprang eagerly followed by the rest; every eye beaming with delight and hope, unconscious as we were, how soon our trials were to commence.*

I soon found that we had landed under very unfavourable circumstances. The sun was intensely hot . . . the country . . . was of a more rocky and precipitous character, than any I had ever before seen; indeed I could not more accurately describe the hills, than by saying, that they appeared to be the ruins of hills; composed as they were of huge blocks of red sandstone, confusedly piled together . . . and so overgrown with spinifex and scrub, that . . . one or other of the party was continually slipping and falling . . .

4

. . . the difficult nature of the ground, which we had to cross, rendered our progress slow and oppressively laborious. A feeling of thirst and lassitude, such as I had never before experienced, soon began to overcome all of us.

Within a few hours, two dogs with the adventurers had dropped dead in their tracks from heat prostration. After temporarily getting lost in a series of steep ravines, the party staggered back to the coast late in the afternoon, exhausted and thirsty.

An inlet, several hundred yards wide, barred their way back along the shoreline to their waiting ship. Some Aborigines were observed on a clifftop across the water. To avoid being caught out overnight without water, Grey decided to swim across the estuary, where the tide was running out rapidly. He instructed his men to wait until he returned for them in a ship's boat.

Grey recorded: *From the rugged nature of the shore I could not have walked a yard without shoes, so I kept them on, as well as my shirt and military cap, and I took a pistol in one hand, as a means of defence against the natives . . .*

I plunged in, and very soon found myself caught in a tideway so violent, that resistance to its force . . . appeared at the moment hopeless. (I should state that the rise and fall of tide here is thirty-eight feet.) My left hand, in which I held the pistol, was called into requisition to save my life; for the stream washed the cap from my head, and the cap then filling with water, and being carried down by the strong current, the chin-strap caught round my neck and nearly throttled me . . . whilst the loose folds of my shirt being washed out to seawards by the tide, kept getting entangled with my arm. I grew weak and faint, but still swam my best, and at last I providentially reached a reef of rocks, which projected from the opposite shore . . .

Grey at last regained his ship in darkness "worn out, naked, and defenceless".

A base camp was set up a few days later near a waterhole, in a position "not being within reach of missiles thrown from the cliffs". A wise precaution on Grey's part, because a number of tribesmen later appeared on the cliffs and hurled down rocks at the invaders.

Some goats and sheep were landed and Grey recorded: *We here first hoisted the British flag, and went through the ceremony of taking possession of the territory in the name of Her Majesty and her heirs for ever.*

Savage biting green ants proved more troublesome than the Aborigines, until the explorers learned not to shake trees while standing under them. They were amazed to see walking fish on the muddy mangrove swamps.

When his camp was established and all stores had been brought ashore, Grey despatched his ship to Timor, to purchase ponies for his proposed overland journey to Perth. His shore party consisted of nine men.

On 17th December, 1837, Grey set out on a preliminary probe of the surrounding countryside. He was accompanied by two companions, each provided with rations for ten days. The party shot pigeons and pheasants for the pot. They observed kangaroos and "opossums" but didn't manage to shoot any. Rain plagued them. They encountered several recently abandoned aboriginal camps and from other signs deduced they were wandering in a well-populated area.

On 22nd December, Grey wrote: *We had just gained the top of a range when a violent storm of rain overtook us. I therefore doubled back about a hundred yards to the left of our former track, to gain some rocks forming a portion of a detached group upon a table land, and which I had observed as we passed them.*

Scarcely had we reached these rocks, and sheltered ourselves under the overhanging projections, when I saw a savage advancing with a spear in his right hand, and a bundle of similar weapons in his left; he was followed by a party of thirteen others, and with them was a small dog not of the kind common in this country. The men were curiously painted for war, red being the predominant colour, and each man carried several spears, and throwing stick, and a club. Their chief was in front, and distinguished by his hair being of a dark red colour from some composition with which it was smeared; the others followed him close, noiselessly, and with stealthy pace, one by one, whilst he, crouching almost to the earth, pricked off our trail.

We remained concealed and motionless until they had all passed, but the moment they came to where we had turned off, they discovered our retreat, and raised loud shouts of triumph, as, forming themselves into a semicircle, they advanced upon us, brandishing their spears, and bounding from rock to rock.

It was in vain that I made friendly signs and gestures, they still closed upon us, and to my surprise I heard their war-cry answered by a party who were coming over the high rocks in our rear . . .

Our situation was now so critical that I was compelled to assume a hostile attitude. I therefore shouted in answer to their cries, and desiring the men to fire one at a time, if I gave the word, I advanced rapidly, at the same time firing one barrel over their heads. This had the desired effect. With the exception of one more resolute than the rest, they fled on all sides, and he, finding his efforts unavailing, soon followed their example.

Grey and his two companions returned to their base camp after this encounter, arriving in time for the Christmas Day celebrations, when "we drank the Queen's health——the first time such a toast had been given in these regions". New Year's day, 1838, was celebrated by the planting of various fruit and vegetable seeds such as barley and potatoes in and round the camp.

On 17th January, Grey's ship returned, bringing with it 26 ponies, 14 goats, 8 sheep and some coconut and breadfruit trees. The livestock did not thrive; and within a few weeks, goats, sheep and ponies began to die. Rain fell almost daily, turning the countryside into a quagmire.

Realizing the wet season would soon begin, Grey set out with some of his men and the remaining 19 ponies late in January, bound for the hinterland. Progress was painfully slow, and by 11th February the party had travelled less than twenty miles. On that day, Grey and two companions scouted ahead of the main party for some miles.

6

One man's job was to blaze trees for the rest of the men to follow. Grey sent him back a short distance to mark a large tree. He wrote: *Finding the man remained absent longer than I had expected, I called loudly to him, but received no answer, and therefore passed round some rocks which hid the tree from my view to look after him. Suddenly I saw him close to me breathless, and speechless with terror, and a native with his spear fixed in a throwing stick, in full pursuit of him; immediately numbers of other natives burst upon my sight; each tree, each rock, seemed to give forth its black denizen, as if by enchantment.*

A moment before, the most solemn silence pervaded these woods; we deemed that not a human being moved within miles of us, and now they rang with savage and ferocious yells, and fierce armed men crowded round us on every side, bent on our destruction.

There was something very terrible in so complete and sudden a surprise. Certain death appeared to stare us in the face . . .

As soon as I saw the natives around me, I fired one barrel of my gun over the head of him who was pursuing my dismayed attendant, hoping the report would have checked his further career . . . My shot stopped him not; he still closed on us, and his spear whistled by my head; but whilst he was fixing another in his throwing stick, a ball from my second barrel struck him on the arm, and it fell powerless by his side. He now retired behind a rock, but the others still pressed on . . .

A spear grazed the explorer's back. Another chipped wood from his gun stock. One of his companions handed him his loaded rifle and Grey stepped out from cover to face his enemies. *I had not made two steps in advance when three spears struck me nearly at the same moment . . . I felt severely wounded in the hip, but knew not exactly where the others had struck me. The force of all knocked me down, and made me very giddy and faint, but as I fell, I heard the savage yells of the natives' delight and triumph; these recalled me to myself, and, roused by momentary rage and indignation, I made a strong effort, rallied, and in a moment was on my legs; the spear was wrenched from my wound . . . and I advanced again steadily to the rock.* (Behind which one of his attackers hid.) *The man became alarmed, and threatened me with his club, yelling most furiously; but as I neared the rock . . . he fled . . . dodging dexterously, according to the native manner of confusing an assailant and avoiding the cast of his spear; but he was scarcely uncovered in his flight, when my rifle ball pierced him through the back, between the shoulders, and he fell heavily on his face with a deep groan.*

The effect was electrical. The tumult of the combat ceased; not another spear was thrown, not another yell was uttered. Native after native dropped away, and noiselessly disappeared. I stood alone with the wretched savage dying before me, and my two men close to me behind the rocks, in the attitude of deep attention; and as I looked round upon the dark rocks and forests, now suddenly silent and lifeless, but for the sight of the unhappy being who lay on the ground before me, I could have thought that the whole affair had been a horrid dream ...

Grey soon after collapsed from his wounds and was later carried back to his main camp and attended by the expedition's surgeon. It was more than two weeks before he was on his feet, limping badly. Grey wrote: *My recovery was a good deal delayed by the circumstances in which I was placed——the heat in the store-tent, a portion of which I occupied, was sometimes as high as 136 degrees of Fahrenheit and ... I had been able to obtain nothing to eat or drink but damper, and tea without sugar; I also reclined upon the ground, until sores broke out from lying on so hard a surface, in one position.*

There were now only 14 surviving ponies. Grey gave up his plan to push southwest to Perth. Instead, he contented himself with minor excursions inland, discovering the Glenelg River in the process. His farthest journey covered approximately 90 miles, along the jagged ridges between the Prince Regent and Glenelg rivers. On these trips, Grey and his party discovered some tracts of fertile country, but they were small in relation to the total area explored. He was greatly impressed with the scenery, wildlife and vegetation, though plagued by almost constant rain. It was now late in March, 1838. In one valley he discovered several acres of wild oats, growing six feet high. Grey and his men ate the grain and found it nourishing.

The explorer, still weak from his spear wounds and in constant pain, had to be lifted on and off his horse, but stoically pressed on with his wanderings inland along the Glenelg. On 26th March, Grey made an extraordinary discovery. In a shallow sandstone cave he found strange, brightly coloured paintings, unlike any other aboriginal artwork discovered before or since. Grey wrote in his journal: *... on looking over some bushes, at the sandstone rocks which were above us, I suddenly saw from one of them a most extraordinary large figure peering down upon me. Upon examination, this proved to be a drawing at the entrance to a cave, which, on entering, I found to contain, besides, many remarkable paintings.... the cave ... was thirty-five feet wide at the entrance, and sixteen feet deep ... Its height in front was rather more than eight feet, the roof being formed by a solid slab of sandstone, about nine feet thick, and which rapidly inclined towards the back of the cave, which was there not more than five feet high.*

On this sloping roof, the principal figure which I have just alluded to, was drawn; in order to produce the greater effect, the rock about it was painted black, and the figure itself coloured with the most vivid red and white. It thus appeared to stand out from the rock; and I was certainly rather surprised at the moment that I first saw this gigantic head and upper part of a body bending over and staring grimly down at me ...

Its head was encircled by bright red rays, something like the rays which one sees proceeding from the sun, when depicted on the sign-board of a public house ... inside of this came a broad strip of very brilliant red . . . the face was painted vividly white, and the eyes black, being however surrounded by red and yellow lines . . .

Upon the rock which formed the left hand wall of this cave, was a very singular painting, vividly coloured, representing four heads joined together. From the mild expressions of their countenances, I imagined them to represent females, and they appeared to be drawn in such a manner, and in such a position, as to look up at the principal figure which I have before described; each had a remarkable head-dress, coloured with a deep, bright blue, and one had a necklace on. Both of the lower figures had a sort of dress painted with red . . . and one of them had a band round her waist.

Grey went on to describe several other paintings, then noted: *The number of drawings in the cave could not altogether have been less than from fifty to sixty, but the majority of them consisted of men, kangaroos, &c: the figures being carelessly and badly executed, and having evidently a very different origin to those which I have first described.* Outside another cave near by, Grey discovered an unusual rock carving. *. . . we observed the profile of a human face and head cut out in a sandstone rock which fronted the cave; this rock was so hard, that to have removed such a large portion of it with no better tool than a knife and hatchet made of stone, such as the Australian natives generally possess, would have been a work of very great labour. The head was two feet in length, and sixteen inches in breadth in the broadest part; the depth of the profile increased . . . to the centre where it was an inch and a half . . . the whole of the work was good, and far superior to what a savage race could be supposed capable of executing.*

In another cave, twenty feet deep, seven feet high and forty wide, Grey found the most unusual painting of all. He wrote: *The principal painting in it was the figure of a man, ten feet six inches in length, clothed from the chin downwards in a red garment, which reached to the wrists and ankles; beyond this red dress the feet and hands protruded and were badly executed.*

The face and head of the figure were enveloped in a succession of circular bandages or rollers . . . These were coloured red, yellow and white; and the eyes were the only features represented on the face . . . The figure was so drawn on the roof . . . it was totally invisible from outside. The painting . . . had the appearance of being much more defaced, and ancient, than any of the others which we had seen.

Here Grey appended a footnote: *This figure brings to mind the description of the Prophet Ezekiel:* "Men portrayed upon the wall, the images of the Chaldeans portrayed in vermilion, girded with girdles upon their loins, exceeding in dyed attire upon their heads, all of them princes to look to, after the manner of the Babylonians of Chaldea, the land of their nativity." *– Chap. xxiii 14, 15.*

The unique paintings discovered by Grey have been generally accepted by Australian anthropologists as aboriginal in origin. They are known as Wondjina figures, after an aboriginal legend concerning ancient visitors to the area, whose spirits remained as paintings on cave walls after their bodies had departed.

The identity of those mysterious early visitors to the northwest coast is shrouded in the mists of antiquity. But it is known that between the 1st and 5th centuries A.D., the Persians and others traded by sea with the islands of South East Asia (the Spice Islands of the Portuguese, Dutch and British a thousand years later).

The flowing robes and rounded, cotton headgear of Persian and other Middle Eastern traders could have inspired the Wondjina paintings in northwest Australia. If Persian ships reached Indonesia, it is possible that one or more landed on the Kimberley coast. Future archaeological expeditions may solve the mystery of the Wondjina cave figures.

Sir Arthur Elliott-Smith, one-time professor of Anthropology at Manchester University, caused much controversy in the 1920s when he put forward the theory that Egyptian seamen visited the Timor sea, off northwest Australia, round 2,000 B.C.

Grey and his party returned to their waiting ship on 15th April, released their 11 surviving ponies and set sail for the Isle of France, two days later. Grey recuperated from his wounds on the island and eventually sailed on to Perth.

His notes on the natural history of the west Kimberley area contain a wealth of interesting observations. One entry concerns a type of dog, other than the dingo, that Grey observed in the area. It was invariably domesticated, and was seen in and around aboriginal camps. Of this dog, Grey wrote: *The new species of dog differs totally from the Dingo . . . I never saw one nearer than from twenty to thirty yards, and was unable to procure a specimen. Its colour is the same as that of the Australian dog, in parts, however, having a blackish tinge. The muzzle is narrow, long, thin, and tapers much, resembling that of a greyhound, whilst in general form it approaches the English lurcher. Some of the party, who went to Timor (for the ponies), stated it to resemble precisely the Malay dog common to that Island, and considered it to be of the same breed; which I think not improbable.*

Grey also recorded sighting the tracks of a very large animal with a divided hoof, almost certainly a buffalo. He noted: *I have still to record the remarkable fact of the existence, in these parts, of a large quadruped, with a divided hoof; this animal I have never seen, but twice came upon its traces. On one occasion, I followed its track for above a mile and a half, and at last altogether lost it in rocky ground. The footmarks exceeded in size those of a buffalo, and it was apparently much larger, for, where it had passed through brushwood, shrubs of considerable size in its way had been broken down, and from the openings there left, I could form some comparative estimate of its bulk. These tracks were first seen by a man of the name of Mustard, who had joined me at the Cape . . . he told me that he had seen the spur of a buffalo, imagining that they were here as plentiful as in Africa. I conceived, at the time, that he had made some mistake, and paid no attention to him until I afterwards twice saw the same traces myself.*

Malay proa ashore on the northwest coast. A variety of Asian seafarers fished the Kimberley waters and traded with the Aborigines for centuries before the arrival of Europeans. Some Chinese arrived in 560 BC. Middle-east navigators may have been earlier visitors

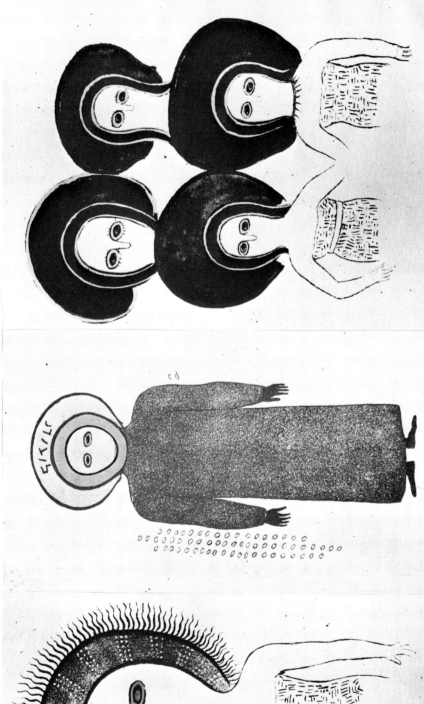

near the Glenelg River where he found unique paintings of robed figures

Cave paintings discovered by explorer Grey, as they appeared in his journal. They are commonly described today as Wondjina figures but their origin remains obscure

A map of "New Holland" made in 1663. Such maps changed little for more than a century

Dampier's map of his voyage in 1699-1700

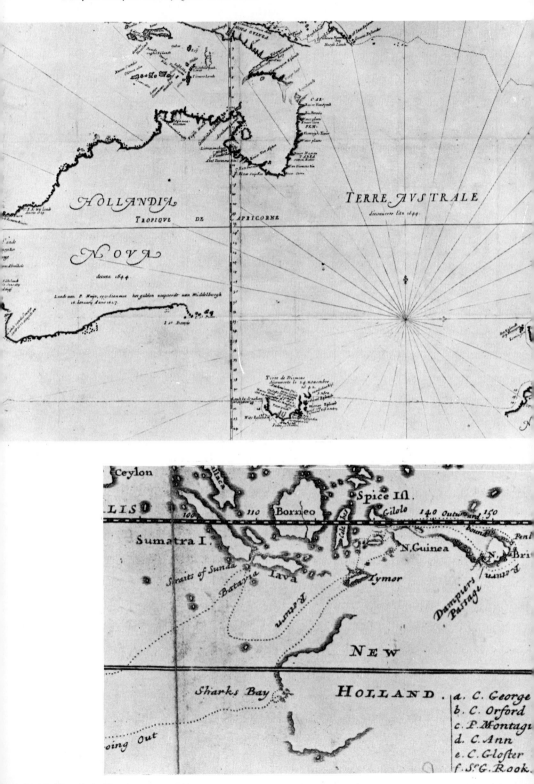

Alexander Forrest, the Kimberley explorer who turned land agent

Sir Frederick Napier Broome, Governor of Western Australia in the 1880s

Sketch of the port of Cossack in the 1880s. The town was established in 1864 by the northwest's pioneer sheep graziers. Pearling started here, but after 20 years the local beds were exhausted and the luggers moved north to Broome. Cossack today is a ghost town of substantial stone buildings. The proposed new mining port at near-by Cape Lambert may boost Cossack as a weekend resort

A sketch of the port of Wyndham in the 1880s. This is how it looked when the pioneering grazing families such as the Duracks and MacDonalds were establishing their grass empires. Modern Wyndham remains tiny and is best known because it is Australia's hottest town

Pioneer settlers returning to the town of Roebourne in the 1880s. The vista is not much changed today

Grey recorded the presence of emus in the area and one "alligator" (crocodile) was sighted in Hanover Bay. Turtles were plentiful, as were kangaroos and bird-life. Concerning the aborigines, Grey made an interesting observation: *A remarkable circumstance is the presence amongst them of a race, to appearance, totally different, and almost white, who seem to exercise no small influence over the rest. I am forced to believe, that the distrust evinced towards strangers arose from these persons, as in both instances, when we were attacked, the hostile party was led by one of these light-coloured men.* (Captain King, in the *Mermaid*, also reported light coloured men he thought to be of Malay origin, on the north Kimberley coast at Vansittart Bay and again in Roebuck Bay.)

In 1839, Grey landed at Shark Bay, near the Gascoyne River (the present site of Carnarvon), and explored the coastline south to Perth. As he travelled largely in whaleboats, he saw little of the inland.

While Grey was travelling down to Perth, the survey ship *Beagle* under Captain J.C. Wickham, examined the northwest coastline of what is now the Northern Territory. This was also in 1839, the year Port Essington (near Darwin) was founded. After visiting the infant port, Wickham took the *Beagle* southwest, discovering the entrances to the Adelaide and Victoria rivers. The surveyor on board was John Lort Stokes, whose published journals later aroused considerable interest in Australia's northwest.

Augustus Churchman Gregory made a brief examination of the Champion Bay area (now Geraldton), in 1846. He stayed only three days. In 1848, he led what was called "The Settlers' Expedition", to the same area, to seek out additional pastures for the expanding livestock population round Perth. He reported finding 225,000 acres of land suitable for sheep grazing near Champion Bay and a further 100,000 acres on the Irwin River, suitable for grazing or agriculture.

In 1857, Frank Gregory, a brother of Augustus, landed at Gantheaume Bay and traced the Murchison River inland for several hundred miles. The following year, after rain had brought up fresh feed for his horses, Frank Gregory was able to push north from the Murchison River to the Gascoyne River. He did this by following the river inland in a northeasterly direction several hundred miles, then making across country northward toward the Waldburg and Teano ranges. The season was good, with plenty of temporary waterholes and creeks. Gregory and his men crossed the Gascoyne and reached the headwaters of the Lyons River near Mount Augustus (named after Frank's brother, Augustus Gregory).

Near the mountain, the explorers surprised an aboriginal camp and made a grisly discovery. Gregory noted: *We here met with strong evidences of the cannibalism of the natives; at a recently occupied encampment we found several of the bones of a full-grown native that had been cooked, the teeth marks on the edges of a bladebone bearing conclusive evidence as to the purpose to which it had been applied; some of the ribs were lying by the huts with a portion of the meat still on them . . .*

Having been in the field just over seven weeks, with provisions remaining for only a further three weeks, Gregory and his men turned back near Mount Augustus. They reached a sheep station on the Irwin River almost three weeks later. After a rest of several days and reprovisioning, they pushed on south to Perth, where they arrived on 10th July, 1858. They had travelled almost 2,000 miles in 107 days.

Gregory reported between 30,000 and 40,000 acres of land near the mouth of the Gascoyne as suitable for settlement, but concluded: "... there is no land worth occupying for many years to come to the west of the Lyons River." (The Lyons is a northern tributary of the Gascoyne, at the mouth of which Carnarvon now stands.)

Gregory's accounts showed the total cost of the six-man expedition to be $80, a modest sum, even in those days.

In 1861, Frank Gregory set out on a much more grandiose expedition, backed by the Imperial and Colonial treasuries to the amount of $8,000. His charter was to explore the northwest coast and hinterland of what is now the Pilbara area. The preamble to Gregory's published journal of this expedition states: *The important additions to geographical discovery, and the large extent of valuable pastoral country that had been found on the Gascoyne River and its tributaries, attracted the attention of a number of English capitalists interested in cotton manufactures, which were then in a very depressed condition in consequence of the civil war in America; it was proposed to establish a new colony on the north-west coast of Australia, having for its special object the cultivation of cotton.*

The nine-man party sailed on the barque *Dolphin* to Nickol Bay during April-May, 1861. This is near the present site of Port Samson and Cossack. After discovering and naming the Maitland River, Gregory and his men headed southeast, where they found a much larger stream, which they named the Fortesque. This was near the present site of Millstream station. A line of hills running parallel with the river to the south was named the Hamersley Range.

After following up the Fortesque for several days, the explorers tried to push southward into the Hamersleys. They penetrated a deep gorge from which they had to retreat when their way was blocked by towering cliffs. This is now called Wittenoom Gorge. Gregory pushed south until he was in sight of Mount Augustus, crossing and naming the Ashburton River in the process. Then he retraced his steps into the Hamersleys, where he climbed and named Mount Bruce, near present-day Mount Tom Price. The party then struck back for the coast, reaching it near the mouth of the Fortesque River, off which stands Barrow Island (now known for its oilfield).

After a few days' rest, the party headed northeast along the coast, crossing and naming the Harding, Sherlock and Yule rivers. Gregory then decided to push inland, following a course parallel with that of the Yule. Then he travelled overland to the north, discovering first the Shaw River and then the De Grey. Veering inland to the southeast, the explorers discovered what they thought was another river, which they named the Oakover (it was in reality the upper De Grey). Gregory then tried to push farther inland from the Oakover into the Great Sandy Desert. He and his men almost

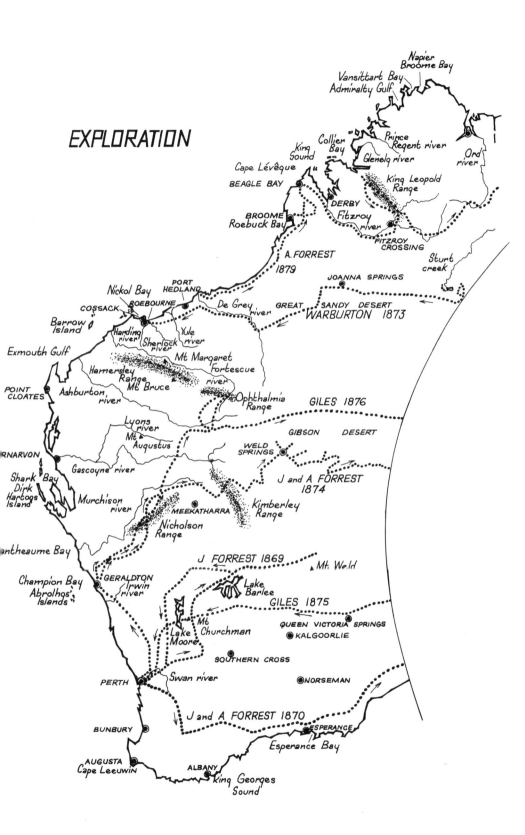

EXPLORATION

Napier Broome Bay
Vansittart Bay
Admiralty Gulf
Prince Regent river
Ord river
King Sound
Collier Bay
Glenelg river
Cape Lévêque
King Leopold Range
BEAGLE BAY
DERBY
Fitzroy river
BROOME
Roebuck Bay
FITZROY CROSSING
Sturt creek
A. FORREST 1879
JOANNA SPRINGS
PORT HEDLAND
Nickol Bay
De Grey river
GREAT SANDY DESERT
COSSACK
ROEBOURNE
WARBURTON 1873
Barrow Island
Harding river
Sherlock river
Yule river
Exmouth Gulf
Hamersley Range
Mt Margaret
Fortescue river
Mt Bruce
Ophthalmia Range
GILES 1876
POINT CLOATES
Ashburton river
Lyons river
GIBSON DESERT
Mt Augustus
WELD SPRINGS
RNARVON
Gascoyne river
J and A FORREST 1874
Shark Bay
Dirk Hartogs Island
Murchison river
MEEKATHARRA
Kimberley Range
Nicholson Range
ntheaume Bay
J FORREST 1869
Mt. Weld
Champion Bay
Abrolhos Islands
GERALDTON
Irwin river
Lake Barlee
GILES 1875
QUEEN VICTORIA SPRINGS
Mt Churchman
KALGOORLIE
Lake Moore
SOUTHERN CROSS
PERTH
Swan river
NORSEMAN
BUNBURY
J and A FORREST 1870
ESPERANCE
Esperance Bay
AUGUSTA
Cape Leeuwin
ALBANY
King Georges Sound

perished on this sortie, struggling back to their depot on foot, after abandoning their horses and equipment. (Gear and horses were eventually recovered.) This country was later crossed, from the opposite direction, by Colonel Peter Warburton, in 1873. Warburton, too, almost lost his life and was saved by two members of his party going ahead 200 miles to bring back help for their collapsed leader.

After their narrow escape, Gregory and his men traced the De Grey River down to its junction with the Shaw. Seven miles downstream from this point, camp was made. Gregory and two companions set out to climb a hill three miles westward, in order to take some compass bearings. Gregory wrote: *Our journey, however, turned out to be fruitless, the magnetic attraction of the volcanic rocks of which the hills are composed being so great as to reverse the needle, which varied so much that I could not even make use of the compass to take angles . . .* (The great iron mining centre of Mount Goldsworthy is located in this area, a few miles to the north of the De Grey River.)

On the delta of the De Grey River, Gregory assessed 100,000 acres of alluvial land suitable for agriculture. The party then followed a course parallel with the coast, east toward the waiting barque *Mermaid* in Nickol Bay. They reached the ship on 17th October, 1861, having been in the field five months.

Writing of the activities of the crew of the *Dolphin* during the ship's long wait in Nickol Bay, Gregory recorded: *Amongst other discoveries during our absence was a bed of pearl-oysters at the head of the bay, from which the crew had procured several tons of very fine mother-of-pearl, besides a small number of pearls varying in size from one to four carats.*

This haul was later valued at $1,000. One of the pearls was estimated to be worth $50. Gregory mentioned in his summary of the journey that he had seen "the Adansonia, or gouty-stemmed tree of Sir George Grey, nearly allied to the baobab or monkey bread-fruit of Southern Africa". Baobabs are rare in the Pilbara today. He reported between 2 and 3 million acres of land suitable for grazing and 200,000 acres suitable for agriculture. Referring to this land, he wrote: *What it appears more highly qualified for than anything else is the growth of cotton . . . From my personal observation of the cultivation of this plant in Egypt . . . I feel confident that a very considerable portion of the arable lands on the De Grey and Sherlock are precisely the soils adapted for the production of this valuable commodity.*

Today, approximately 110 years after Gregory's visit, the land he thought suitable for agriculture still awaits the plough.

The far hinterland of the New Frontier was first penetrated by John Forrest, later to be Premier of Western Australia and architect of the bold Kalgoorlie water pipeline scheme. In 1869, with his brother Alexander, he ventured inland via Lake Barlee to the Laverton area. Here Forrest mapped and named Mount Flora, Mount Margaret and Mount Weld. A near by peak, clearly shown on his map, he did not name. Today it is known to the world as Mount Windarra, scene of the fabulous Poseidon nickel mining boom.

14

In 1874, John and Alexander Forrest set out from Geraldton to cross through the centre of the continent to the Overland Telegraph-line, hoping to reach Charlotte Waters, or the Finke, south of what is now Alice Springs. Following the upper Murchison River inland to the Meekatharra district, they veered north to Weld Springs, then southeast, just missing Lake Carnegie. After many hardships, they won through to explorer Gosse's recent tracks in the Musgrave Ranges, south of Ayers Rock, and pressed on to the telegraph line, reaching it a few miles north of Charlotte Waters. The journey took the party six months and was an epic of endurance.

No discoveries of useful land were made, for grazing or agriculture. Nor did the brothers report any indication of promising mineral areas, except by a map reference to "micaceous iron ore" in some hills near Meekatharra, which Forrest named the Kimberley Range. Before setting out on his momentous but fruitless journey, John Forrest had received a letter from the surveyor-general of Western Australia, Malcolm Fraser, who confidently advised him that he was headed for "another land of Ophir" (land of gold). Ironically, gold was later discovered in several of the areas visited by Forrest; but neither he nor his brother Alexander reported any sign of this precious mineral.

The Forrest brothers' major discovery was that all the vast hinterland of the New Frontier was arid, inhospitable and scarcely fit for human habitation. No subsequent discoveries have been made to refute this judgement. Apart from a handful of mining and pastoral outposts, the country inland from Kalgoorlie, Wiluna and the Oakover remains uninhabited.

Two years after John and Alexander Forrest had crossed from Geraldton to the Overland Telegraph-line, explorer Ernest Giles repeated the marathon journey. He travelled a roughly parallel course, about 100 miles farther north. Leaving Geraldton in March, 1876, Giles and his small party headed northeast for more than 500 miles to the Tropic of Capricorn. When Giles reached this point, he was suffering acutely from ophthalmia and became temporarily blind. With a fine sense of drama, the explorer named a line of hills the Ophthalmia Range. His second in command, Alec Ross, described an outstanding peak to the northwest, which Giles named Mount Robinson. Close by the Ophthalmia Range, which Giles could not see himself, was the formation now known as Mount Whaleback, the outcropping backbone of a buried colossus of iron ore. Today the modern town of Newman stands where Giles once found only rocks, spinifex and sand.

Looking east toward their distant goal, Ross described to Giles a scene of open, sandy desolation to the horizon. The explorers retreated to their base camp on the headwaters of the Ashburton River, near a picturesque gorge Giles had named Glen Ross. After resting, the party thrust eastward toward what Giles had named, two years earlier, the Gibson Desert. They eventually won through to the Overland Telegraph-line, having traversed even worse country than that encountered by the Forrest brothers. Giles, too, reported only desolation and utterly useless country. To this day, the route Giles followed for more than 500 dreadful miles is completely uninhabited to the Northern Territory border.

Alexander Forrest explored the Kimberley region in 1879. He landed at Cossack on 3rd February with his brother Matthew, four other Europeans and two Aborigines. The party had 26 horses and rations for six months. The plan was to examine the coastal country as far north as the Glenelg River on Collier Bay, then proceed directly across country to the Overland Telegraph-line. (In 1866, Alexander McRae had briefly explored the Fitzroy River from its mouth in King Sound.)

The season was good, with plenty of water and feed for the horses——but the expedition was almost wrecked in the early stages by hordes of tormenting grey mosquitoes! The explorers reached Beagle Bay, north of present-day Broome, on 9th April, after two months of almost sleepless nights. There they were surprised to find two pearling boats, belonging to captains Patterson and Munro. The enterprising Forrest chartered one of the boats for a brief trip to the near-by Lacepede Islands.

The explorers then rode to the southeast, rounded King Sound at the mouth of the Fitzroy River and headed inland into rough, hilly country. Forrest named the low but rugged and inhospitable peaks, the King Leopold Range, after King Leopold of Belgium. The country proved impenetrable for the horses, so after reaching Collier Bay, Forrest more or less retraced his steps to the Fitzroy River, which he then followed up-stream to the east.

Near the junction with the Margaret River, and beyond to Hall's Creek, the party found large tracts of good grazing country. Then they crossed the vast, richly grassed Nicholson Plains to the Ord River. The last leg of the journey, eastward of the Victoria River, took the adventurers into dry waterless country. Starving and thirsty, they reached the Overland Telegraph-line and rode wearily into Katherine station on 29th September, 1879.

The aftermath of Alexander Forrest's Kimberley exploration was rather more interesting than the journey itself. Both he and his brother John Forrest were accused in the Western Australian parliament of using information gained during their work as government surveyors to their own advantage. One Member, Thomas Campbell Carey, claimed the brothers jointly held more than 1.2 million acres of leasehold land.

This was not substantiated and it seems Alexander Forrest's only immediate reward for his Kimberley exploration was a lease of 5,000 acres near Derby, on what is now Yeeda station. However, early in 1880, less than six months after his return, he left his government job and set up as a land agent in Hay (then Howick) Street, Perth.

Forrest advertised in newspapers that he would give advice, for a fee, to intending Kimberley pastoralists and speculators. Within three years, 51 million acres had been leased in the northwest, mostly by speculators hoping to sell their leases at a profit. Many of these deals were handled by Alexander Forrest, who acted also as agent for a number of genuine settlers such as the MacDonalds, Duracks, Costellos and Emanuels.

In 1883, the Western Australian authorities sent John Forrest to survey the town sites of Broome and Derby and to report on the country explored by his brother. Alexander accompanied John Forrest, in an unofficial capacity. The Kimberley country apparently didn't fire John Forrest's imagination as vividly as it had Alexander's——his official report somewhat pricked the boom started by his brother and much of the speculation in leases fizzled out.

Before the new wave of mineral exploration began in the 1960s, Giles and the Forrest brothers had been regarded as the last explorers of the New Frontier. Now, after a century of neglect, the remotest corners of the northwest are being examined afresh. Fantastic treasures of minerals have been discovered — and the final chapter of exploration perhaps remains to be written.

Settlement

The first European settlement on the northwest coast was made by Walter Padbury on the Harding River, near what is now Roebourne. Padbury decided to settle in the area after reading Frank Gregory's favourable report of his 1861 expedition.

With several employees, Padbury landed near the present ghost town of Cossack from a chartered ship *Tien Tsin* in April, 1863. The settlers brought with them 450 sheep, 7 horses, a team of working bullocks, tools and rations. There was no suitable grazing land in the tidal swamps round Cossack, so Padbury and his men explored up-stream towards Roebourne for a suitable place to settle. They found this near a stand of wild nut trees, at a place that became known as "the Walnuts".

Several other settlers followed Padbury within a few months. One was John Wellard, who arrived on 18th August, 1863, with 370 sheep, 26 cattle and 9 horses, and established Andover station. His manager, Shakespeare Hall, had been one of Frank Gregory's exploring party, in 1861. Walter Padbury later established a grazing property farther north, on the De Grey River; but this venture failed and he brought his stock back to the Roebourne district.

In 1864, the first women settlers arrived. They were Mrs John Withnell, whose first name was Emma, and her sister, Fanny Hancock (an ancestor of present-day mining magnate, Lang Hancock). John Withnell decided to take up land near Roebourne for grazing.

He brought with him 1,050 sheep, 10 draught horses, 10 cattle and a variety of tools, stores and equipment. His party (apart from his wife and sister-in-law), included his two young children, his brother-in-law, John Hancock, Robert Withnell and two employees.

Things, at first, did not go well for the new settlers. They arrived on the chartered schooner *Sea Ripple* at Cossack in April, 1864. The vessel had been becalmed for two days before they finally landed, then temporarily stranded on a small island surrounded by muddy tidal creeks. When the tide went out, the ship was left lying on its side at a dangerous angle. Stock and passengers had to scramble ashore over the mud. The sun was hot, there was no shade, and the settlers were tormented by flies, sandflies and mosquitoes. The only water was in the ship's kegs. The party found itself stranded several days until another tide rose high enough to float the schooner off. Meanwhile, the ship had sprung a leak and repairs had to be made with canvas and tar. Most of the stock died, from drinking salt water.

Eventually the *Sea Ripple* drew into Cossack on 8th April, 1864. There was no settlement at that time, so the party stowed their goods and pitched camp on what seemed to be high ground. For several days the men explored the Harding River, looking for grazing land and fresh water. When they found a good site, near what is now the town of Roebourne, they returned and brought the women and children.

Most of the horses and cattle were dead, so everyone carried what they could in their hands or on their shoulders. Most of the supplies had to be left behind, to be brought up later. It was a long and weary walk for the women in the stifling tropical heat, to the new camp-site. Emma Withnell carried one of her sons and led the other by the hand. The group reached the shady trees and pool of water at their journey's end, and here Emma named a small near-by hill "Mount Welcome".

When the men returned to Cossack next day for the remainder of their goods, they found that these had been swamped and washed away by an exceptionally high tide, driven in by a gale. Crates of food, clothing and other goods had been swept out to sea. Only heavy items such as tools, harnesses, ammunition and guns remained, plus some flour, tea and salt — though a lot of it sodden. Of the stock only 86 sheep, 1 horse and 1 cow survived.

Eventually the settlers established themselves in huts built of stone and mud, thatched with spinifex and other grass. Stone proved a good choice of building material, because the settlers discovered that cyclones were frequent on this part of the coast.

In September, barely six months after they had landed, the industrious, determined settlers sheared their first wool clip and sent away 10 bales, hand-washed by Emma Withnell and Fanny Hancock.

The following year, 1865, Roebourne began to boom. A resident magistrate, several policemen, post office officials and other government representatives arrived; but a number of public buildings were only half-completed when a cyclone blew up and the rising town was destroyed by wind and rain.

John Withnell and his family were left homeless, but they quickly erected a larger, more substantial homestead. Two years later, they lost all their savings (148 gold sovereigns) and the season's wool clip when the vessel *Emma*, bound from Cossack to Perth, went down in a cyclonic storm. All 42 people on board were never seen again.

Three other ships, bound for or leaving Cossack, went down in the same year. About this time, smallpox broke out in the district, killing many of the aboriginal population. The settlers blamed Malay prawn and beche-de-mer fishermen for bringing this disease to the northwest coast.

Emma Withnell, using what medicines she had, nursed several Malays and her own children through the epidemic. Eventually the Withnell fortunes changed, and the settlers moved inland to a larger grazing property at Sherlock.

John Withnell was a man of some ingenuity as well as dogged industry. He is said to be the first man to use a canvas water (cooling) bag. He was among the first Europeans on the northwest coast to go "beach-combing" for pearl shell — for a while more profitable than sheep grazing.

By 1870, Roebourne was on the way to becoming a busy, prosperous little town. Cossack was officially declared a town and port in 1872. In that year, Roebourne was again flattened by a bad cyclone. The Withnell flocks were reduced from 6,000 to 1,200 and again their homestead was destroyed.

After that, all public buildings in Roebourne and Cossack were constructed of heavy blocks of stone; most were completed in the late 1880s. A bank was set up in Roebourne, and tram-line for horse-drawn vehicles linked the two settlements in 1887. Gold was discovered 200 miles inland at Nullagine, in the same year.

By then, many thousands of square miles of grazing country inland from the two towns had been settled. Among the pioneer "hinterlanders" were Frank and E. H. Wittenoom, the Lacey brothers and the Darlut family. The country they settled for grazing is now known for its mining products. The port of Cossack, the town of Roebourne and the linking tram-line were kept busy supplying, transporting and selling all kinds of goods, machinery and supplies to the hinterland.

The tram carriages were fitted with padded seats placed lengthwise down the centre of the vehicle, so that the two rows of passengers sat back to back. Red and white striped curtains kept out the sun, and the driver sat in a partly enclosed seat at the front of the tram. There were two passenger trams and one goods tram daily from both Roebourne an Cossack.

Point Samson, nearer to the tip of Cape Lambert than Cossack, also developed as a port. In an exposed position, the jetty was washed away several times in cyclones. (An iron ore port is to be built near Point Samson on Cape Lambert.)

Cossack became a colourful place, with a polyglot population, mostly connected with the pearling industry. The luggers were European-owned, the crews largely malays and seamen from Manila. There were also a number of Chinese in the town, a few Japanese men and more Japanese women. The population of Cossack's Chinatown, 150, trebled when the pearling fleet had its annual "lay-up" during the off season. There were three Chinese stores, a Chinese bakery, a Japanese store, a Turkish-bath house and a Cingalese tailor.

Many public works such as road building, at Roebourne and Cossack, were carried out by aboriginal prisoners, chained together in pairs. They were fitted with leather-bound collars, attached to a light mesh chain about ten feet long. The prisoners worked and slept in their chains, which were linked together in "strings" when they were shifted from place to place.

Most workers on the early pastoral properties in the area were indentured

Aborigines. This was the legal description of the system under which they worked; but it was, in fact, a form of slavery. The Aborigines after signing an agreement they scarcely understood, found themselves completely in the hands of their employers. With very few exceptions, no wages were paid, except in the form of "keep". This was usually one pound of flour and one pound of meat a day, plus two pounds of sugar and a quarter pound of tea weekly. Clothing was supplied, mostly cast-offs from the European community. An Aborigine's wife and children also received rations, but they were expected to work when needed.

One severe critic of the indentured labour system, Archbishop Rily, wrote to the Governor of Western Australia: *This is only a form of slavery, as the natives for the most part do not know what it means and for the rest do not dare to refuse to sign the agreement. As soon as a man is indentured he is absolutely under the power of his master, and just as some masters treat their animals well and others treat them badly — so is the treatment of natives.*

When it was suggested that aboriginal workers should get more pay, the pastoralists of the time said they could not afford this since the Aborigines were unprofitable to employ, because of their laziness and their costly habits of "riding horses to death" and "cutting sheep" (in the shearing).

These arguments were still being used in the late 1960s, though pastoralists had managed to survive profitably, over the previous one hundred years! ("Slow worker" clauses were written into labour Acts in the Northern Territory and Western Australia, as recently as 1968.)

A year after Cossack and Roebourne were founded in 1864, an attempt was made to settle Roebuck Bay, the present site of Broome. This venture was organized by Sir F. P. Barlee, who formed a pastoral company in Perth. The first shipment of his company's sheep went ashore early in 1864, under the care of two settlers, Panter and Harding, who were accompanied by constable Goldwire and others. (Panter, with another man named Martin, had previously explored the Kimberley coast between Roebuck Bay and Hanover Bay, where George Grey landed.) The sheep did not thrive; Panter, Harding and Goldwire were murdered by the Aborigines, and the settlement abandoned in 1867.

In the same year that the ill-fated Roebuck Bay settlers landed, another attempt at settlement was made farther north, at Camden Harbour — this venture organized by a group of Victorian colonists who were, to say the least, ill-prepared for the undertaking. A writer of the 1880s told the story:

Following close upon the attempt to settle Roebuck Bay, came the disastrous expedition to Camden Harbour, a locality beyond the Fitzroy between Collier Bay and Prince Regent's Inlet, visited by Sir George (then Captain) Grey, and again in 1862 by Dr Martin. These explorers both wrote in raptures of the country around Camden Harbour, which Dr Martin, in particular, described as the finest in Australia. Acting upon their information, a Victorian, Mr William Harvey, conceived the idea of forming a company to settle the land of so much promise, and in 1864 a party of eighty-four persons — consisting of painters, plumbers, slaters, saddlers, a doctor, a clergyman, but with scarcely anyone experienced in stock, and not a shoemaker, blacksmith, or carpenter amongst them — sailed in three vessels from Hobson's Bay for this distant destination. Shortly after reaching it, they were joined by the late Mr R. J. Sholl as resident magistrate, with whom came a staff of surveyors, police and pensioners. Difficulties and disappointments dogged the footsteps of these unfortunate pioneers. Want of water was encountered in the first place, then want of feed — the coarse, rank grass, heated by tropical suns, proving innutritious and wholly unsuitable for sheep. To a poison plant, also, quantities of their stock fell victims, while fever and sun-stroke carried off several of the men. Their troubles were crowned by the dangerous hostility of the natives, and, thoroughly disheartened by a succession of misfortunes, the settlement, in 1865, was finally abandoned, some of the shareholders returning to Melbourne, and others proceeding south to Nickol Bay.

In its one year of operation, all the Camden Harbour Pastoral Association's 4,500 sheep died or were lost. Many of the Victorian colonists who took part in the venture, were lured by a somewhat misleading prospectus, which stated that Camden Harbour was only 270 miles north of Perth. The harbour was, in fact, more than 1,500 miles from Perth.

Inspired by Augustus Churchman Gregory's glowing description of the Denison Plains, which he discovered in 1855, another Melbourne group, the Denison Plains Association, was formed to attempt a settlement in the northwest, in 1865.

With only a hazy notion of where the Denison Plains were located, the colonists set out from Melbourne to sail to Roebuck Bay. They intended to then ride to their "Promised Land", near the present Northern Territory-Western Australian border. This would have involved crossing 500 miles of inhospitable, unknown country.

At Fremantle, the settlers became disheartened to learn of the failure of the Camden Harbour venture. They pressed on to Cossack, where they were becalmed off shore and ran short of water. On learning that the Roebuck Bay settlement had been abandoned, following the murder of Harding, Panter, and Goldwire, the colonists gave up their plan to reach the Denison Plains. Instead, they settled briefly on the Maitland River, about 50 miles west of Cossack and not far from the present iron port of Dampier. The venture failed, after much squabbling, and was abandoned early in 1866.

Some of the investors in the Denison Plains and Camden Harbour associations claimed they had been swindled and wanted to know what had happened to the $80,000 invested in the two organizations. They never found out.

While the various land-development schemes foundered, the pearl-shell industry was thriving. A contemporary writer summarized the history and current state of pearling, with special reference to the part played by Aboriginal divers:

Mr Pemberton Walcott (who had accompanied Frank Gregory on his explorations of Nickol Bay), discovered those pearl-shell beds which subsequently became the basis of an extensive and profitable industry. At first, the value of Walcott's find does not seem to have been fully appreciated, though beach-combing to a small extent was early carried on. A man named Tays, an American sailor, was the principal pioneer of an industry in which the labour of the natives was eventually utilised to the great advantage of both blacks and whites. This man, and after his death by drowning, his partner Seubert and others, gathered the shells at first in shallow water, or at low tide. When the beach beds became exhausted, they encouraged the natives to wade into greater depths and "bob under" for the shell. By this means the blacks were gradually taught to dive, and in 1868 a first experiment in boat-diving was made with much success, while in the following year this practice was generally established. Landsmen, who had chief command of native labour, were soon drawn into the business . . . The natives employed in pearling by the pastoral firms were almost invariably well treated . . . But pearlers who were not pastoralists began to appear upon the scene when the profits of the business became known. These men . . . sometimes found a difficulty in procuring the divers they required, and were not always sufficiently particular in the methods they adopted for supplying their wants. "Nigger hunting" among the wild blacks became not unknown, nor other practices decidedly irregular.

The position of the Aborigines in the first 25 years of white settlement in the northwest was well expressed by a writer in the 1880s. He recorded: The blacks of the Nor'-west were a fine, strong, and numerous race. At Nickol Bay, save in one case of treachery — sternly punished — they gave but little trouble, though farther south on the Ashburton, and later again on the Gascoyne, they remained hostile and dangerous for years. What proved their safeguard was the need of the settlers for their services. Only by means of cheap black labour were many of the latter able to carry on their enterprise. Instead, therefore, of internecine hostilities arising, as so often has elsewhere been the case, it was in the interests of the Nor'-western settlers to gain the confidence and goodwill of their sable neighbours, and to attach them to their stations and homesteads. The natives were soon taught to shepherd, to shear, to ride, and even to fence, drive teams, and perform station work for which whites elsewhere are invariably employed . . . The government, laudably desirous of preventing even the suspicion of wrong-doing in the relations between the whites and blacks, early began a course of legislation regulating contracts for native labour, and elaborately protecting the interests of Aborigines. These efforts, however well meant, have had in some respects an injurious effect . . . The substitution of a complex contract system for the simple patriarchal relations which formerly existed between the squatters and the tribes whose "country" they severally occupied, has been productive of anything but satisfactory results. While the blacks looked upon themselves as dependents of the white "master" who had settled upon their lands, while they ate his flour, drank his tea, smoked his tobacco, wore his blankets, and unhesitatingly obeyed him as a child would do the bidding of a father, fancying in their simplicity that he had authority over them, and quite content that it should be so — all went well. But when the

Government stepped in and taught the natives to consider themselves free agents, beyond the control of the squatters unless they bound themselves to him by a special contract, the old peaceful order of things was seriously disturbed, the blacks in too many cases turned insolent and idle, and their relations to the whites previously all that could have been desired, became correspondingly strained.

Following Alexander Forrest's successful exploration of the Kimberleys in 1879, speculators and settlers began taking up large tracts of land between the Fitzroy and Ord rivers.

A year earlier, in 1878, Bishop Gibney of Perth had tried, and failed, to establish a mission station at Disaster Bay in the Kimberleys.

In 1882, fossickers Adam Johns and Philip Saunders, found small quantities of alluvial gold near the headwaters of the Margaret and Ord rivers.

Lured by Alexander Forrest's report of 25 million acres of rich grassland in the Kimberleys awaiting settlement, several New South Wales grazing families decided to look at the new country. They were the Duracks, the Costellos, the Emanuels, the Kilfoyles and the MacDonalds. The first four families were in partnership, having extensive properties throughout Queensland, as far west as Cooper Creek — the MacDonalds, from Goulburn, southwest of Sydney, on their own.

In 1881, the head of the Durack family, Patrick and his brother Michael, sailed to Perth where they talked with Alexander Forrest about the land he had discovered. Forrest was then a prosperous land agent for the area. As a result of this meeting, the Duracks applied for a number of large grazing blocks along the Ord, Negri, Margaret and Fitzroy rivers and on the Nicholson Plains. The total area they reserved was round two and a half million acres — subject to a personal inspection of the land. The selections were made largely in the name of Durack, Emanuel and Kilfoyle.

The Duracks sailed home to Queensland and organized an expedition to inspect their new lands. This required the chartering of three ships: one to take the men, horses, equipment and rations to Darwin, another to take them on from Darwin to Cambridge Gulf and another to pick them up on the west coast at Beagle Bay. Michael Durack led the six-man party. They took twenty-three horses, two of which died on board in the various mishaps of the voyage. (Their first ship was wrecked soon after leaving Brisbane and they had to return overland and charter another.)

Eventually the party got ashore in Cambridge Gulf in August, 1882, near what they hoped was the entrance to the Ord River. The river, however, was not the Ord, and the surveyor in the party, John Pentecost, named it the Durack. Farther up-stream, a large river joining the Durack was named the Pentecost.

After many trials and tribulations, the party reached the junction of the Negri and the Ord, which they recognized from Forrest's description. From there they followed the explorer's track westward to the Fitzroy, and on to Beagle Bay. Some miles before striking the coast, they arrived at Yeeda station, a sheep grazing property established by George Julius Brockman (from the Roebourne area), in 1880. They were told that other sheep properties were being established along the Fitzroy, including Meda, Lulagai and Mundoona, all running between two and four thousand sheep.

At Beagle Bay, the explorers had to wait three weeks for the ship they had chartered to take them home. Eventually it arrived and Durack and his men sailed south to Fremantle, then round the southern coast to Sydney, arriving in January, 1883, after six months' absence.

In June and July 1883, four large mobs of Durack cattle set out from western Queensland, bound for the Kimberleys. The total number was 7,520 head, plus 200 horses and 60 working bullocks. In all, 22 men went on the track with the cattle, some of them going only part of the way, to be replaced by others.

The Emanuel family, headed by Solomon Emanuel, elected to stock the land they had taken up with sheep, instead of cattle. These were shipped to Derby and walked inland to the Emanuel properties on the flood plains of the Fitzroy River and the adjoining spinifex and pindan country bordering the Great Sandy Desert.

While the Durack cattle were on the track westward, another pioneer drover, Nat (Bluey) Buchanan, took a large mob belonging to a Melbourne pastoral company to a newly-acquired holding on the upper Ord River. Buchanan was the original pioneer of the stock-route across the Top End of the Northern Territory, having taken cattle over to the Victoria River in 1878. In 1883 he was accompanied by Tom Cahill and some Gordon men, who had been with him on some of his earlier Territory adventures with men like Sam Croaker, D'Arcy Uhr, John Costello, and Bob Button.

A month before the Durack cattle set off on their odyssey, another big mob had set out from Goulburn, in N.S.W., bound for the junction of the Fitzroy and Margaret rivers, 3,500 miles away. These cattle belonged to the MacDonald and MacKensie families.

Of the thousand beasts that started on this terrible trek, just a few head completed the journey. Only one of the four MacDonalds who set out from Goulburn reached the Fitzroy — Willie MacDonald. To make good the drought losses to his herd, he bought more cattle along the way, in western Queensland and the Northern Territory. He eventually arrived in the King Leopold Range country near present-day Fitzroy Crossing with several hundred head of cattle, and here established Fossil Downs station, in 1886.

The Durack cattle finally reached the Kimberleys late in 1885. The nightmare journey had cost 4,000 head, two men's lives and $140,000 (including the stock losses). On the marathon journey, 1,300 calves had been born along the track, but all had to be destroyed because they were unable to walk with the mob. The surviving 3,500 cattle were used to stock Lissadell, Argyle and other Durack properties, plus Tom Kilfoyle's adjoining Rosewood station.

Meanwhile, other Duracks had arrived by ship, near the mouth of the Ord in Cambridge Gulf, and set up a store. In addition to rations and general supplies they had brought mining equipment with them, following rumours of gold in the

Kimberleys. In the same year, 1885, another store was established by an ex-policeman, August Lucanus, in partnership with a Darwin businessman. They hoped to do a brisk trade with the expected rush of prospectors, after publication of a report by the Western Australian government geologist, Edward Hardman.

In 1886, more gold rumours were spread by a colourful, garrulous Kimberley pioneer, William Carr Boyd. In company with William O'Donnell he surveyed a property on the lower Ord for an eastern pastoral company. This work completed, he spread exaggerated stories of gold finds, then charged eager prospectors arriving in Cambridge Gulf two dollars each for directions to the "goldfields". Not much gold was found, though several thousand diggers combed the Kimberleys as far afield as Hall's Creek. A few made good, but what little alluvial gold they found didn't last long. Many prospectors died of starvation and fever, or were speared by the Aborigines.

Up-stream from the Durack and Kilfoyle properties, Buchanan's partner Bob Button had established Ord River station for an eastern pastoral company. The cattle were brought across a year earlier from Wave Hill, on the Victoria River in the Northern Territory. While the legendary "Bluey" Buchanan had returned east to bring over another mob in the same year as the Duracks and MacDonalds, Button had taken the cattle across to the Ord in Western Australia. He was almost certainly the first overlander to reach the northwest, though Buchanan had accompanied him to within 200 miles of his final destination.

In 1886, a year after the Duracks and ex-policeman Lucanus set up their stores on the shores of Cambridge Gulf, the embryo settlement was officially declared the Port of Wyndham by John Forrest, Premier of Western Australia.

More stations were established throughout the Kimberleys, and prospectors continued to arrive from all parts of the world. The first woman to arrive in the northwest came overland from the Northern Territory with Afghans and a string of camels, to establish a shanty pub at the Hall's Creek gold diggings, late in 1886. She gave her name as the "Mountain Maid" and travelled on to the Nullagine diggings when the brief Hall's Creek rush ended.

In November, 1886, John Durack was speared to death by Aborigines near the border of Argyle and Rosewood stations. Angry settlers organized a "punitive expedition". No records of that expedition were kept, but camp-fire stories, passed down through the generations, suggest that many Aborigines, young and old, male and female, were shot down to avenge the death of one white man.

For the next twenty years, there was an unreported twilight guerilla war between the invading white men and the dispossessed black men. Old police records and private papers recorded only a fraction of these protracted hostilities, but they make grim reading. Published letters and newspaper stories of the time indicate that many of the new settlers considered that "the only good Aborigine is a dead one".

One of the better-documented stories of the "black war" in the Kimberleys concerned a tribesman named Sandamara. He was accused of cattle spearing in his

"In Paddy Hannan's Day" — a photo in the Golden Mile Museum, Kalgoorlie

Paddy Hannan (left) the man who started Western Australia's biggest gold-rush — to Kalgoorlie, in 1893

American cattlemen at a sale in the Kimberleys

Derby's high school was the first centre of secondary education in the Kimberleys

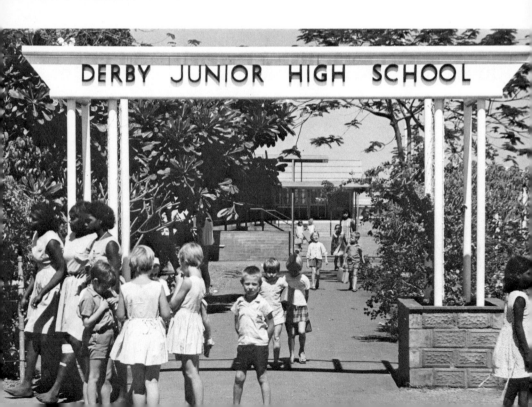

A young nickel miner and his wife at Kambalda

Residents of the iron mining town of Tom Price in the Pilbara region

A typical Pilbara miner — hard-hatted, bearded and plum-coloured from ore dust

A young mother in the modern shopping centre of the company town of Tom Price

Single men's dining room in one of the Pilbara mine towns. Labour turnover is high among single men. Mining companies provide excellent and cheap housing for families, in an effort to maintain a stable work force. Single men are used chiefly for construction work and other temporary jobs. Permanent positions in mines, workshops and railways are reserved where possible for married applicants. (W.A. government photo)

Western Australia's Minister for Industrial Development and the North West, Charles Court (second from left) at a Pilbara mine opening ceremony

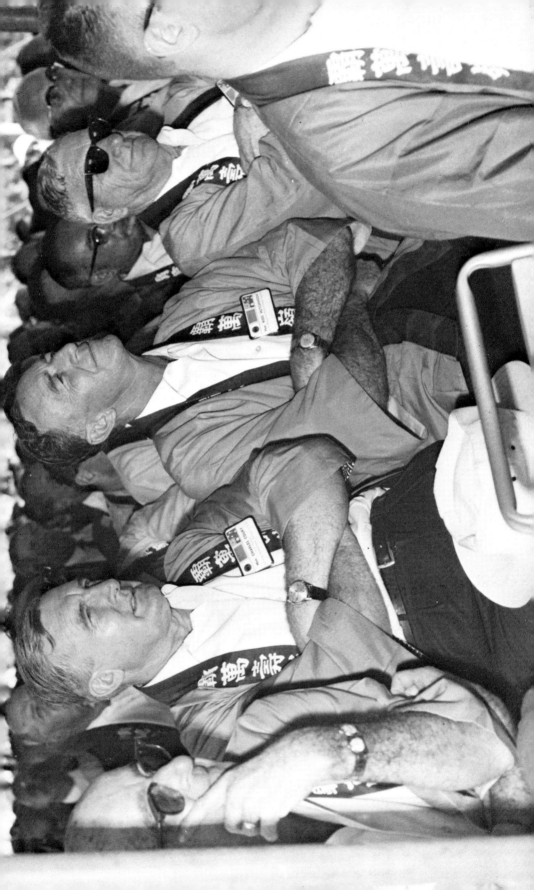

REG. OFFICE OF....

HANCOCK & WRIGHT

HANCOCK PROSPECTING PTY. LTD.

WRIGHT PROSPECTING PTY. LTD.

E.A.WRIGHT & CO.

PILBARA EXPLORATION NO LIABILITY

NUNYERRY ASBESTOS COMPANY

RAGGED HILLS LEAD MINE

RAGGED HILLS PTY. LTD.

GEORGINA HANCOCK (1965) PTY. LTE

HANCOCK (PILBARA) PTY. LTD.

HANCOCK (NICKEL) PTY. LTD.

WRIGHT (NICKEL) PTY. LTD.

MICHAEL WRIGHT

JULIAN WRIGHT

Wolf Creek Crater, south of Hall's Creek, not far from the junction of the
Canning and Bililuna stock routes (W.A. government photo)

Aerial view of the Top Dam construction town, near Kununurra on the
Ord Scheme (W.A. government photo)

Aboriginal shoppers in the main street of new Hall's Creek

Shire offices in Kununurra. Well-designed modern buildings, shade trees and a park-like atmosphere are a feature of this well-planned village

Graziers yarn outside the pens at a Kimberley cattle sale. New breeds are improving the quality of the district's stock

A road-train loaded with cattle bound for Derby crosses the Fitzroy River near the tiny settlement of Fitzroy Crossing

Here, 3rd June 1885
the MacDonald brothers of Goulburn N.S.W, halted
their waggon, completing the worlds longest droving
trip to stock Fossil Downs with cattle from their
Clifford Downs Station, Laggan, N.S.W, whence they
set out on Easter Monday 1882

Their bullock waggon was the first vehicle to cross
the Australian continent from East to West, and this
tyre from a rear wheel commemorates their exploit

Set in position by the Hon. Lady Gairdner on the
70th. anniversary of their making camp at this spot

Widow Mrs William MacDonald with her daughter outside Fossil Downs homestead at the hub of her million-acre domain

The author's vehicle crossing the Margaret River on Fossil Downs station

Supplies being unloaded at Wyndham jetty

One of the district's few exports — geological samples

tribal territory on the Lennard River, where white men had established Lilmalura station. Sandamara was gaoled in Derby, and while in custody, was trained to be a "police boy". He was given the white-man name of "Pigeon". (Other popular names for black men were "Quartpot" and "Sugar-bag".)

When his sentence was completed, Sandamara accompanied many police patrols through the Kimberleys. These expeditions usually had the one purpose: to apprehend tribesmen accused of spearing sheep or cattle. Many of the Aborigines undoubtedly did this, regarding themselves as free to hunt any animals on what they considered was still their own tribal country. As the herds grew bigger and trampled down or consumed the natural cover of the indigenous wildlife, there was often nothing else for the Aborigines to hunt.

Using a local Aborigine to track down his own people in his own tribal country was not typical of the period. Usually "police boys" were used many miles from their own tribal lands, in "foreign" country where they had no friends or relations and were regarded by the local Aborigines as interlopers, to be punished, often by death, if the opportunity arose. Thus the police became the protectors of their "boys", who stuck close to them, worked well and never deserted, because of their fear of the consequences of being caught by the local tribesmen.

The much-publicized loyalty of "police boys" was motivated largely by fear, rather than gratitude to the white men who had brought them into strange country far from their tribal lands.

Why this rule was disregarded in Sandamara's case is not clear, but it was to have disastrous consequences for both black and white.

On one long patrol Pigeon accompanied constable Richardson from Derby into his home country. The journey lasted several months and sixteen of Pigeon's countrymen were apprehended on charges of cattle spearing. The prisoners were captured in twos and threes as the weeks went by, each being chained by the neck to the growing string. The first men caught spent hundreds of weary miles in their chains, trudging behind their mounted captors.

Toward the end of the patrol, on their way home to Derby, constable Richardson, Pigeon, another tracker called Captain and the sixteen prisoners camped at abandoned Lilmalura station. This was Pigeon's tribal land. The sight of his countrymen crouched miserably in their chains, facing years of prison for hunting in their home territory, apparently stirred him to rebellion. Perhaps it was the jibe of "traitor" from one of the chained prisoners? No one knows.

In the night, Pigeon and Captain shot constable Richardson to death and released their countrymen. Then the eighteen renegades made off, taking with them three rifles and three revolvers. They decided to make war on the white man, and ambushed a wagon in the King Leopold Ranges to obtain more arms. The attack took place in Winjana Gorge, where two white men, Francis Burke and Oswald Gibbs were murdered. A third white man, Fred Edgar, and two aboriginal stockmen escaped.

27

Following this second outrage, Pigeon and his band were pursued all over the Kimberleys for several years, by police patrols and privately organized "punitive expeditions". During the hunt for Pigeon, many settlers considered any Aborigines as fair game. Men, women and children were shot down indiscriminately.

Police records of raids on aboriginal camps by superintendent Lawrence, constable Pilmer, constable McDermott, constable Blythe, constable Spong, all of whom led separate parties, indicate that 38 innocent Aborigines were shot dead in the course of official investigations. Another 16 men, including Pigeon and his accomplices, were also shot, by sub-inspector Drewry and some of the constables already mentioned. Seven captured Aborigines were taken to Derby and hanged or sentenced to life imprisonment.

Many of the innocent Aborigines were shot in Geikie Gorge, now a tourist attraction near Fitzroy Crossing. Pigeon was killed near Tunnel Creek in the Napier Range, not far from Leopold Downs station.

Remarks in some of the official reports and other contemporary writings indicate that many more than the published "tally" of Aborigines — men, women and children — died during the search for Pigeon.

Meanwhile, Nat Buchanan and his son Gordon had established Sturt Creek and Flora Valley stations. The MacDonald clan had settled in at Fossil Downs, and their tenacity of purpose and doggedness lived on there. In the 1970s, the widow Mrs William MacDonald was still in charge of the million-acre property and its 20,000 cattle.

In the 1880s and early 90s, other pastoralists whose names were to become household words in the Kimberleys established their empires. They included such pioneers as Connor, Doherty, Emanuel, Streeter, Male — many still important names on the New Frontier's northern borders.

Development

Growth of the towns

Cossack, the first permanent town established in the northwest, did not thrive after the turn of the century. Broome, a better-situated port, became the centre of the pearling industry that began round Cossack. Roebourne, only a few miles inland from the pioneer harbour, became the northwest's major business centre and town.

Cossack's only claim to fame in the last years of the 19th century was that it boasted the first motor car in the wild northwest. This was driven round the tiny port, late in 1898 and 1899, by Miss Ada Stewart, daughter of the licensee of the Weld Hotel. Bicycles were very popular among the youths of the town at that time, so Cossack could possibly claim to be the pioneer of modern transport in the northwest.

Cossack also had a meatworks, where as many goats as cattle were killed, to supply local butcher shops. Hope in the ailing port's future briefly revived when a turtle-soup factory was established, to supply a supposedly strong market in France. After raising $4,000, the entrepreneur sailed for France to find out exactly what sort of soup the Parisians most preferred. Apparently he didn't return and the venture lapsed.

By the 1960s, Cossack was a ghost town of abandoned, roofless stone buildings and crumbling wharves. In 1970, the Western Australian Government announced a plan to spend more than $20,000 refurbishing some of the port's historic buildings, to attract tourists – the old town may have a future, as a resort.

Roebourne fared only slightly better than Cossack; though not abandoned, it did not thrive. By the 1960s Roebourne was a sleepy town, with a handful of commercial premises, police station, post office, hotel, school and homes for a population of a few hundred. However, development of Cape Lambert as an industrial area and port, serving the Robe River-Mount Enid iron mines, may revive Roebourne.

The port of Broome, after an abortive attempt at settlement in 1864, eventually became a permanent town in 1883, when John Forrest and others took up land for cattle grazing in the area. (Previous attempts at sheep grazing had failed.) Pearling luggers, working the surrounding waters, began to call in regularly; and by 1887, Broome was the centre of the pearling industry. A submarine cable linked Broome with Java in 1889.

The resident population became and remained largely Asian; Japanese and Malays predominated, with a number of Chinese, Filipinos, Aborigines and Europeans. Broome's peak population in the 1920s of approximately 5,000 included 1,200 Japanese, 600 Koepangers from Timor, 600 Europeans and several hundred each of Chinese, Aborigines, Filipinos, Macassans and Malays.

At that time, 400 pearling boats worked out of Broome; but World War II disrupted the pearling industry and the introduction of plastic materials for button making forestalled a major recovery. Today, only a handful of pearling luggers operate out of Broome, chiefly to supply young living shells for the cultured pearl industry at Exmouth Gulf, Cape Leveque, Kuri Bay and other centres.

A meatworks, established in 1940, and handling up to 40,000 beasts during the April to October season has brought some local employment. A new jetty, more than half a mile in length, provides deep-water berths even at low tide for oversea ships. The old wooden jetty, built in 1897, catered only for smaller vessels, which had to lie on the mud when the tide ebbed.

Although its population has been greatly reduced since the 1920s, Broome's fortunes are no longer declining. It seems assured of a future as a tourist centre and deep-water port for the west Kimberley area. (Derby's new jetty is a quarter of a mile from the sea at low tide.) The expected boost in export-beef sales could considerably brighten Broome's future. Mineral development could also bring prosperity to the west; and drilling operations at Nerrima Dome, Frome Rocks, Poole Range, Price's Creek and at Goldwyer have already produced indications of oil and gas.

Derby became a town in 1883, following the arrival of the first settlers in the district, in 1880. One of the first sheep stations was Yeeda, established by George Julius Brockman, on land originally granted to Alexander Forrest. Other settlers landed sheep at near-by Beagle Bay and later at Derby, for pioneer grazing properties along the Fitzroy, Meda and Lennard rivers. Speculators in Perth and Melbourne took up much of the land by 1880, after negotiations with Alexander Forrest, who set himself up as a land agent. Most of these "map graziers" never saw the land they leased, but merely paid the rent for a time, then sold out to settlers in the area, who wanted more or better land. (Most leases were required by law to be at least 50,000 acres, annual rental being $1 for a 1,000 acres.) Leassees were required to stock their land within a certain period or forfeit their lease. The stocking rate was usually 20 sheep or 2 cattle to 1,000 acres. Between 1880 and 1883, more than 51 million acres were taken up on leasehold. Much land was relinquished by the "map graziers" when it proved worthless, and usable grazing land changed hands a number of times in some cases before it was stocked. A year after Derby was founded, leases covered only about 11 million acres.

The settlement at Derby was no more than a shanty town until the gold-rush of 1883-4 gave it a mild boost. Today Derby has a sprawling suburban area, a sizeable shopping and business centre, and amenities of all kinds. In the 1960s, the first high school in northwest Australia was built in Derby. The district's polyglot population continues to grow steadily, following the extension and improvement of west Kimberley beef properties, and the increasing tempo of mineral exploration. District road development promises employment for the local work force, which includes many Aborigines and citizens of widely mixed races. Development of previously neglected cattle grazing properties also provides a continuing labour market.

Derby has a modern abattoir, built in 1966, where west Kimberley beef is packaged for export. Output is likely to increase in future years. Tourism is another growing local industry. The annual Boab Festival, held in August, features an aboriginal corroboree, a rodeo, and tours of cattle stations.

Huge bauxite deposits have been discovered northeast of the town, near Admiralty Gulf. Closer in, several companies have drilled for oil. Mineral developments may turn Derby into a boom town — but otherwise the long-established coastal town should develop steadily, if not spectacularly.

Inland from Derby, the only settlements are Fitzroy Crossing and Hall's Creek. The first consists of a hotel-motel with a general store attached, police station and hospital. Hall's Creek, as established in 1948, remains raw and ill-sited in the eyes of the visitor. In open, inhospitable, dry country, it has a small hotel, garage, several stores, post office, police station, hospital, school, airstrip and a scatter of homes for the town's 350 citizens. Further tree planting may one day transform the town into a pleasant oasis in the surrounding stone and spinifex semi-desert country.

Old Hall's Creek, ten miles away, is today a ghost town of roofless, crumbling pisé buildings. The creek is usually dry, except for a few long water-holes, shaded by a straggle of ghost gums. Sheets of corrugated iron, rusting machinery, wire and glittering broken glass strew the landscape.

Wyndham, close by the original 1885 Kimberley port of Durack and Lucanus, still awaits its heyday. The port's liveliest boom took place in the 1890s, when Kimberley beef was shipped south to feed the hungry miners on the Kalgoorlie goldfields. But disease, borne by the cattle tick, stopped this trade after a few years.

At the time of federation, 1901, Wyndham's brief prosperity had almost expired. An intermittent export trade in live cattle to Java and Manila kept the small settlement alive until 1919, when a government meatworks was established. For a time the town's future brightened, but low prices and lack of markets stifled any real development. In its best years, the Wyndham meatworks processed about 30,000 beasts. Because of its poor quality, Kimberley beef has not secured high prices — even in the 1960s, its price rarely exceeded half that of dressed beef on the east coast. Recent herd improvements may eventually stimulate a demand for Kimberley beef, and lead to higher prices.

If and when the Ord River Scheme begins to produce export crops, Wyndham may yet have its long-awaited boom. But to date, it remains a tiny, sleepy, tidal port, hemmed in by a soaring, rocky escarpment at its back door and mud-flats only a few hundred feet away, on the other side of the town's only major street.

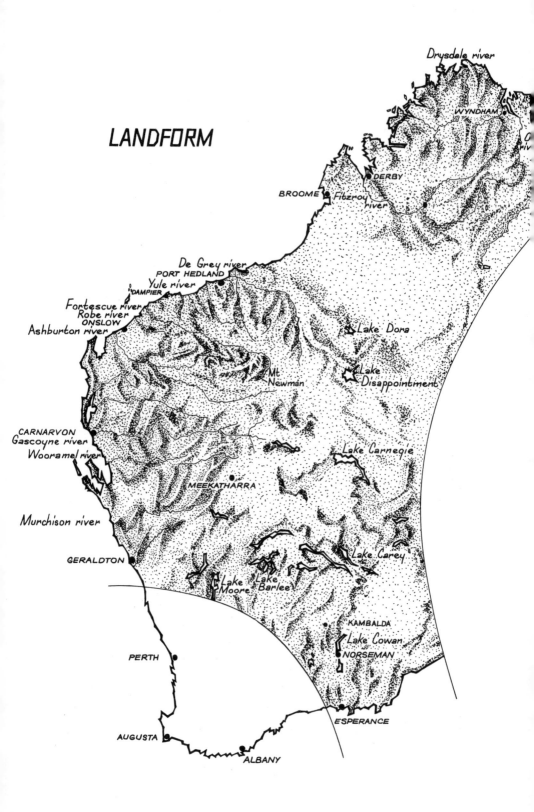

LANDFORM

Drysdale river

WYNDHAM

DERBY

BROOME
Fitzroy
river

De Grey river
PORT HEDLAND
Yule river
DAMPIER

Fortescue river
Robe river
ONSLOW
Ashburton river

Lake Dora

Mt
Newman

Lake
Disappointment

CARNARVON
Gascoyne river
Wooramel river

Lake Carnegie

MEEKATHARRA

Murchison river

Lake Carey

GERALDTON

Lake
Moore
Lake
Barlee

KAMBALDA
Lake Cowan
NORSEMAN

PERTH

ESPERANCE

AUGUSTA

ALBANY

Tourism and some commercial development is taking place up-stream of the present town centre, on the site officially planned (but never used) last century. New buildings at "the three-mile" and "the six-mile" make Wyndham one of Australia's longest towns, as well as the narrowest and hottest. Wyndham has few other attractions.

The northwest's newest town, Kununurra, was established to service the controversial Ord River Scheme. A planned settlement, modelled on Canberra-suburban lines, it has a semi-circular cluster of business and administration premises. All buildings are modern and set among native or planted shade and ornamental trees. Suburban streets radiate from the commercial centre, and are lined with modern tropical homes, many of them built well above ground, on the north Queensland pattern.

Of only village size early in 1970, Kununurra will probably become a sizeable town in the next decade. Unlike most Australian country dwellers, Kununurra's farmers live in town and travel daily to their irrigation blocks. The Ord farmers see more of each other than their counterparts in the south and east, and there is a strong community feeling in Kununurra. Farmers generally, are well-informed on developments outside their own area, including oversea rural trends. Despite the rather stultifying climate, there is a refreshing community vitality in Kununurra not generally encountered in Australian country towns. Americans and other immigrants from advanced oversea rural districts have contributed to this.

The many blank spaces on the present town plan, if filled, could accommodate a much larger population. After completion of the Ord Dam, up to 170,000 acres of irrigated farmland may support a local community of 20,000. Whether this dream will become reality remains to be seen.

Climate will affect the growth of the population, for most of the Kimberley district is north of Cairns, a latitude most Australians consider too hot for comfort. The Kimberley average year-round temperature is 84 degrees Fahrenheit. Winter temperatures range between 70 and 78 degrees. Very little country rises above 2,000 feet, so altitude provides no escape from the heat. Wyndham (not Marble Bar) has the highest annual average temperature in Australia.

The wet season, coinciding with the hottest months (December to April), makes the Kimberley summer period a sore trial to most Europeans, despite air-conditioning. Prolonged outdoor activity is scarcely bearable. The climate is similar to that of the Congo coast and Portuguese southwest Africa.

Near the southern extremity of the New Frontier's coastline, the historic ports of Carnarvon and Geraldton have steadily developed since they were founded last century. Carnarvon, basically an agricultural and fishing port, exports wool, fruit and vegetables. Rich, alluvial river flats — 700 acres in area — are irrigated from wells in the usually dry bed of the Gascoyne River. The district produces crops worth $2 million each year, including bananas, tomatoes and beans. Carnarvon has its own prawn processing factory and the main commercial species handled are tiger and king prawns.

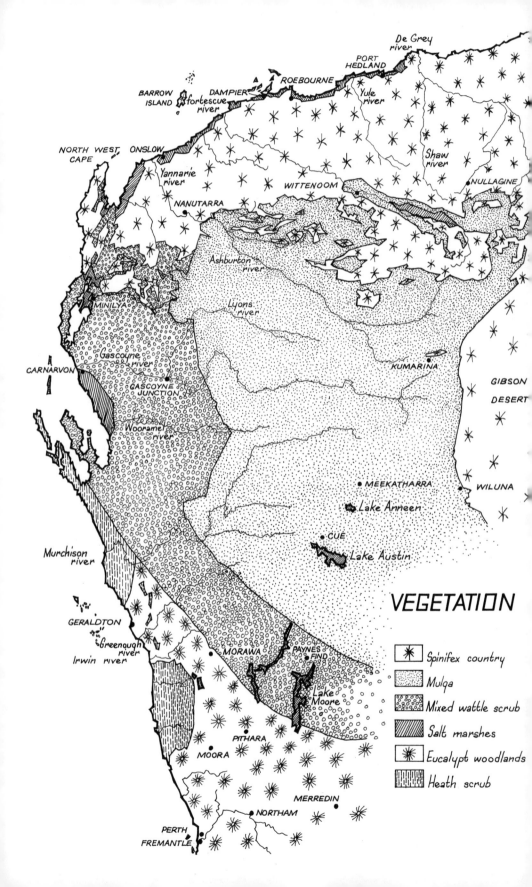

These grow to 11 inches in length and weigh up to 7 ounces. Salmon are also netted in the Carnarvon and Shark Bay areas.

Geraldton was established as a port after the discovery of lead in the Murchison River by Pemberton Walcott, a member of Augustus Gregory's "Settlers' Expedition" in 1848. The State's first surveyor-general, John Septimus Roe, marked out the town site in November, 1849.

The original name for the settlement was Gerald Town, after Governor Charles Fitzgerald, who visited the area for a few days with Augustus Gregory in December, 1848. The Geraldine lead mine, also named in honour of the governor, first shipped lead out of Champion Bay in 1849. Between 1853 and 1856, convicts worked the mine. Australia's first smelting furnace, built at the Geraldine mine in 1855, produced 25 tons of lead each month — some going to Singapore, where it brought $66 a ton.

Western Australia's first government railway, bringing lead to Geraldton from Northampton — a distance of 33 miles — opened in 1879. Geraldton became the port for various coal and gold mining centres and eventually linked by rail with Meekatharra.

A private organization, the Midland Railway Company, built a line 300 miles south to Perth, between 1891 and 1894. This line remained in private hands until 1964, when it became part of the West Australian Government Railways' network.

Gold, copper and other minerals, from the Mount Magnet-Peak Hill area, came to Geraldton via the Meekatharra railway. The line was extended 110 miles eastward to Wiluna, after the discovery of gold, and there a large mine was established, employing hundreds of men. In its heyday, Wiluna's population was around 10,000, and by 1970, this had fallen to less than 50. In 1966, Geraldton became the first port on the New Frontier to export iron ore to Japan. The ore is mined by the Western Mining Corporation at Koolanooka, about 100 miles southeast of the town. This company signed the first contract with the Japanese, for the sale of 5 million tons of ore, to be delivered between 1966 and 1974.

The New Frontier's best known mining towns were established 300 miles southeast of Wiluna, in 1892, following gold discoveries at Fly Flat. Prospectors Arthur Bayley and William Ford winnowed 600 ounces of alluvial gold from dry creek-beds amid the scrub, sand and spinifex. A gold-rush followed, when they turned up with their find in the mining town of Southern Cross.

A wave of prospectors re-christened Fly Flat with its aboriginal name — Coolgardie. Fossickers and adventurers came from all over the world to set up the biggest tent and shanty town Western Australia had ever seen.

Three years later, in 1895, there were 8,000 residents and scores of permanent buildings — some quite substantial. The railway reached the town in 1896, paving the way for a further influx of gold-hungry prospectors. By 1898, the population reached 20,000. There were several banks, a mile of shops, a stock exchange, three daily newspapers, three breweries, a host of other establishments and a growing suburban sprawl. (Herbert Hoover, destined to become President of the United States of America, lived and worked in Coolgardie for a while.) The boom ended in less than a decade, when the alluvial gold began to fizzle out.

Meanwhile, Kalgoorlie was born 25 miles farther inland, following Irishman Patrick Hannan's discovery of gold nuggets there in 1893. By the turn of the century, most of Coolgardie's population had migrated to Kalgoorlie.

An area two miles long by half a mile wide (one square mile) became known as the "Golden Mile". The gold was mostly deep underground in reefs, but the rewards were fabulous for companies with sufficient resources to dig deeply. The area became, and remains, the world's richest square mile of rock. Between 1893 and 1970, the Golden Mile produced 1,100 tons of gold.

Production continues, at the rate of almost 15 tons of gold a year. This is extracted by four major companies operating in the Golden Mile. More than 3,000 men work on the mines, two-thirds of them underground. Although its boom days are over, Kalgoorlie continues to thrive, with a stable population (including the twin-town of Boulder) round 15,000. An additional 7,000 people live in the surrounding shire district.

Grazing is another traditional local industry, with half a million sheep producing about $3 million worth of wool yearly.

Coolgardie today, contrasts sharply with bustling Kalgoorlie, for it is a ghost town. The whole town has been turned into a museum that is an outstanding example of what can be done with a commercially defunct, but historically important centre. Many buildings are being restored and markers along the streets tell the romantic, colourful story of the gold-rush days.

Brightly painted relics of the mining era fill vacant blocks of land between abandoned buildings. Dusty shops, long closed, have window displays of old photos, paintings, bottles and household items of the lamp and buggy era. The old government building has been converted into an imposing museum, crammed with relics of the town's golden era. The only one of the town's 26 hotels still doing business, the *Denver City,* was refurbished in authentic colonial style as a tourist attraction.

One plaque tells of the railway contractor who donated $2,000 for champagne, as part of the celebrations to mark the arrival of the first train. Those were the days! They may come again to the Coolgardie area, now being exhaustively reprospected, following the big nickel strikes at Kambalda to the south, and Windarra in the north.

New mining towns, such as nickel-rich Kambalda, are springing up in the southeast corner of the New Frontier. Farther north, nickel finds by the Poseidon mining company and others promise a new lease of life for the ailing gold towns of Leonora and Laverton.

The sheep farmers

In 1862, the Western Australian Government tried to encourage settlers into the Pilbara region. The exploring Gregory brothers had reported good pastoral and agricultural land on the Murchison, Gascoyne, Ashburton, Fortescue and De Grey rivers.

Grants of freehold land of 100,000 acres were offered to anyone willing to settle in the area. Rent was $1 a 1,000 acres each year. Settlers had to stock their land immediately with at least 200 sheep and fence a portion of their runs within three years. Those who could not afford 200 sheep had to be content with only 50,000 acres!

Walter Padbury, John Wellard, John Withnell and Harold Venn were among the first to take up the Government's offer and settle the Cossack-Roebourne area in 1863-6. After many tribulations they and other settlers established sheep grazing in the Pilbara region.

Early attempts to establish sheep in the west Kimberley area round Broome and Camden Harbour in 1865-7 met with failure, through footrot and other troubles. Eventually the Emanuel family successfully grazed sheep along the lower Fitzroy and Lennard rivers, and westward from Derby to Broome. Today, there are 170,000 sheep in the district, but for the most part, the Kimberley region is almost exclusively cattle country.

The Pilbara by 1867 contained 61 sheep properties, grazing a total of 31,000 animals — 5½% of the State's sheep population.

Isolation, poor country, low rainfall and lack of permanent water were the major obstacles early pastoralists faced. Experience has since proved much of the country unsuitable for grazing, but men driven by pioneering zeal do not readily give up. They are consumed by a fanaticism that will not let them yield or retreat. Many had burned their bridges behind them; having sunk what little they had in their arid, lonely empires, they were condemned to live out their lives on them.

Transport proved a major problem. Everything was carried by sea, on frail ships that were frequently lost in cyclones. Shipping costs were high for livestock, wool, and all kinds of freight.

About 1866, the Western Australian Government offered a rent-free grant of 100,000 acres to anyone who could find a stock-route north from Geraldton to the sheep lands of the Roebourne district. E. T. Hooley pioneered an overland track in the same year. He started with 1,900 sheep from the Champion Bay area on 27th May, 1866, and reached the Roebourne settlement on 23rd August — losing less than a dozen sheep on the 700-mile trek.

Hooley's stock-route was used intermittently for some years, but it was a hard track in dry times. Watering points were widely spaced and not always reliable. When feed was scarce, many sheep ate poison weed and died.

The ruling price for wool in those days was high — 12 pence a pound. But the

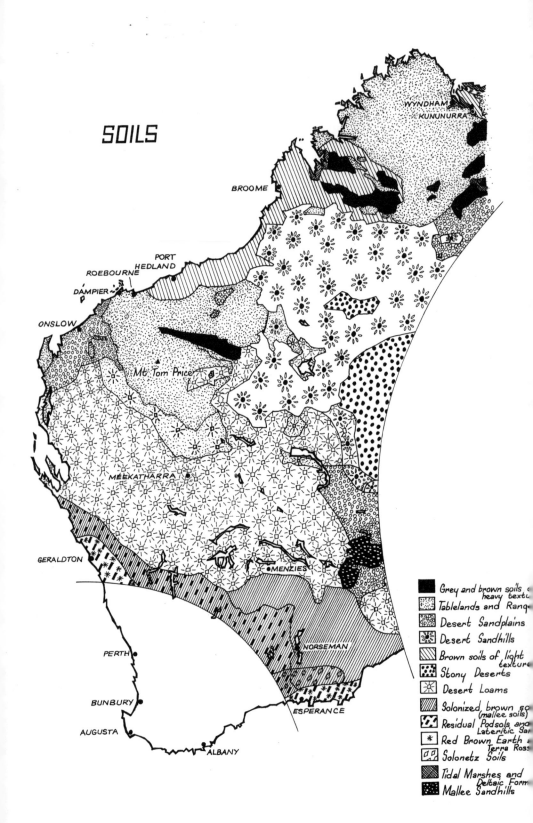

SOILS

WYNDHAM
KUNUNURRA

BROOME

PORT
HEDLAND
ROEBOURNE
DAMPIER

ONSLOW

Mt Tom Price

MEEKATHARRA

GERALDTON

MENZIES

PERTH

NORSEMAN

BUNBURY

ESPERANCE

AUGUSTA

ALBANY

■ Grey and brown soils of heavy textu

Tablelands and Range

Desert Sandplains

Desert Sandhills

Brown soils of light texture

Stony Deserts

Desert Loams

Solonized brown so (mallee soils)

Residual Podsols and Lateritic San

Red Brown Earth a Terra Ross

Solonetz Soils

Tidal Marshes and Deltaic Form

Mallee Sandhills

northwest settlers never received this amount, because of high freight and scouring charges. The red oxide dust of the area made Pilbara wool unmistakably dirty. Pioneer sheepman John Withnell finally succeeded in obtaining 12 cents a pound for his wool, after scouring it by hand before shipping it direct to England.

In 1870, there were 50,000 sheep in the northwest, representing about 8% of Western Australia's sheep population. The average price of wool was 18 pence a pound.

Most of the work on the sheep stations was carried out by aboriginal shepherds. This was necessary, settlers claimed, because they couldn't afford to pay white labour. Convicts and ex-convicts, the only other feasible source of cheap labour, were prohibited by law from entering the northwest. On Pyramid station, inland from Roebourne, a flock of 2,000 sheep was entirely looked after and sheared by Aborigines, who were regarded as reliable, satisfactory workers.

By 1875, the sheep population of the northwest had grown to 105,000 — 12% of the State's sheep tally. In 1890, the number reached a peak of 820,000, or 33% of Western Australia's sheep. After that, the northwest wool industry slumped for nearly 20 years, wool prices fell, and drought ravaged flocks. Smaller stations were swallowed up by large, absentee-owned pastoral enterprises.

Few of the runs were fenced, so amalgamation presented only paper problems. Flocks grazing on the open range changed hands in lawyers' offices in distant Perth without causing a ripple of concern to the uncomprehending aboriginal shepherds and shearers.

Some of the sheep empires built up in this period were enormous, even by Australian standards. The Union Bank controlled over 4 million acres, the West Australian Mortgage Company took over almost 5 million acres, and Dalgety and Company 13 million acres. Alexander Forrest, explorer of the Kimberleys and land agent, reputedly had interests in 1.6 million acres of sheep land.

In the wool slump of the 1890s, various discoveries of gold were made in the northwest, the first at Nullagine River, in 1887. Station hands walked off sheep properties in search of riches on the diggings.

Labour was scarce and those pastoralists who could afford it began fencing their runs so they could manage their flocks without shepherds. (The first sheep-men to fence their properties were Anderson and Grant, in 1878 — but generally, fences were rare on northwest sheep runs until the turn of the century. Subdivision fences are still few and far between, in the 1970s.)

A few pastoralists imported indentured Chinese workers, to avoid paying higher wages to Europeans — who offered to replace the aboriginal shepherds who had absconded to the goldfields. After a while, the Chinese drifted off to the diggings, too.

When they returned, they asked for and received the same wages as Europeans; but the returning aboriginal shepherds did not. In an effort to keep down costs, the pastoralists began finding fault with the quality of black labour (which for the

39

previous 20 years had been highly regarded). They were lazy, irresponsible and slow in all things; when shearing — a job at which they had previously earned praise — it was now claimed they cut sheep. Such inefficiency was hardly worth paying for, so Aborigines were offered only their keep, and rarely any cash for their labour.

Thus commenced the myth of the aboriginal "slow worker". Today, after some 80 years of work-without-pay or minimal wages, near starvation protein-deficient diet and shockingly depressed living conditions, many aboriginal station employees *are* slow workers. The myth has become reality.

The New Frontier's northwest now runs 3 million sheep — 10% of Western Australia's total sheep population. This decline from 33% in 1890 is due largely to pasture degeneration caused by over-grazing. Lack of subdivision fencing and an eagerness to "get the most out of the land" has brought about poor station management.

Scientific research has not substantiated pastoralists' claims that they have been "eaten out" by native animals such as the euro (a type of kangaroo). In fact the reverse has been proved: sheep have eaten out plants of their own preference, leaving only vegetation unpalatable to them, but favoured by euros. Hence the sheep decline, while the euros increase.

Eradication of the euros solves nothing, because their diet consists of plants rejected by sheep. Removal of the sheep, to allow plants they favour to regenerate, is the only answer — together with controlled grazing to make sure the vegetation isn't eaten down to extinction.

It is interesting to note that the 3 million sheep in northwest Australia that have caused widespread land deterioration represent less than 2% of Australia's 170 million sheep. On conservation grounds, a strong case can be made for further reduction of the sheep numbers in northwest Australia.

The cattle kings
By 1888, most of the cattle properties established by the Duracks, MacDonalds and others in the Kimberleys were in serious difficulties. The hoped-for boom round the settlements at Wyndham and Derby had not taken place, and there was no export market for beef, to Asia or the eastern States. The only cattle buyers were local butchers, who catered for the hundreds of prospectors still hopefully ranging the Kimberley area. Most of the easily accessible alluvial gold had been picked up. Unless reef gold could be discovered and permanent mines established, the already dwindling population threatened to vanish as quickly as it had grown.

The Durack family and others formed a mining syndicate called "The Argyle Downs Gold Mining and Quartz Crushing Company". Heavy mining machinery was brought by ship from Sydney to Wyndham and hauled overland to Ruby Creek near Hall's Creek. There was no worthwhile gold, and after a year the venture failed. The machinery was abandoned and still lies rusting under the sky on the outskirts of old Hall's Creek.

Fever, which had plagued the settlers since their arrival six years earlier, in 1883, reached alarming proportions about the time of the mining crash. Stockmen, weakened and fed-up by recurring illness, deserted and returned east with departing miners. Big stations covering hundreds of square miles were left tended by one man, assisted perhaps by an aboriginal stockman from Queensland. Few Kimberley Aborigines worked on the stations — whose ownership they still disputed whenever an opportunity arose.

In the slump of 1889, the local tribes sensed that the white man was disheartened and considered leaving their country. (Scores of Europeans were drifting back to Derby and Wyndham to await ships to take them away.) There was an upsurge of spear attacks on men, cattle and sheep. Fires were lit to burn out the pastures on which the invaders' cattle fed; unguarded store-houses and homesteads raided for food, axes and firearms; travelling stock stampeded; and wagons raided.

The Kimberley pastoralists demanded more police protection and asked for reinforcements to "teach the blacks a lesson". Deputations to Alexander Forrest caused the explorer-turned-land-agent to publicly suggest a punitive expedition of special police "strong enough to resist, subdue and leave a lasting impression on the aborigines".

To their credit, the police in Derby maintained that many of the pastoralists' stories about the depredations of the Aborigines were untrue or exaggerated. They pointed out that as the stations were badly understaffed, many of the stock losses came about through straying rather than spearing or stealing. Dry seasons had also contributed to the reduction in sheep and cattle numbers. (To this day, many thousands of cattle die of starvation in the annual Kimberley dry season, because the grass at this period has a low food value.)

The reluctance of the police to undertake punitive expeditions annoyed the settlers, who took matters into their own hands, whenever they could muster enough guns to raid aboriginal camps.

Local feeling was expressed by Jim Durack in the last lines of a poem dedicated to John Durack, speared by Aborigines:

Ah who shall judge the bushman's hasty crime
Justified both by circumstance and clime?
Righteous the hate with which the soul is filled
When man must slaughter or himself be killed.

The gold-rushes to the southern half of Western Australia in the 1890s provided a brief market for Kimberley cattle. By 1891, Western Australia had attracted only 50,000 settlers, after more than 60 years of colonization; but the lure of gold boosted the State's population to 184,000 by the year 1900.

Alexander Forrest and Isadore Emanuel formed a company to export cattle from their own and surrounding west Kimberley properties. They chartered ships of the Blue Funnel Line and the Adelaide Steamship Company for the transport of stock via Fremantle to the hungry miners on the goldfields, in 1894.

In the same year, east Kimberley cattlemen, Connor and Doherty, formed a similar export company, shipping their stock out of Wyndham. In 1896, the Durack family joined the firm, which became known as Connor, Doherty and Durack Limited. In Broome, the firm of Streeter and Male began exporting cattle from stations inland to the Fitzroy River and beyond. Since losses were high and animals arrived in poor condition, prices were discouraging, and the trade languished.

Small lots of live cattle shipped to Singapore brought even lower prices. From 1891, for a few years there was a small but profitable market for beef in the Northern Territory while 10,000 Chinese toiled on the diggings round Pine Creek.

Redwater fever, which had plagued the Kimberley cattle herds throughout the 1880s, threatened to extinguish the industry in the early 90s. Countless thousands of beasts died, but as the years passed, the survivors built up an immunity to the disease.

Up to the present day, profitable, reliable markets for Kimberley beef have proved hard to find. Some stock went to Darwin for the local trade, but most Kimberley cattle were sold as store beasts to eastern pastoral companies. Mobs were walked overland across the Top End of the Northern Territory into the fattening areas of Queensland.

Only the strongest cattle could stand such treks of over 1,500 miles. Most animals leaving the Kimberleys to walk to Queensland were about six years old, whereas eastern graziers close to markets could send away mature animals under three years of age. This meant, in broad terms, that the annual turn-off of the Kimberley stations was usually only half that of comparable properties in the east. The low prices offered for Kimberley store cattle, because of the expense of overlanding them, further reduced the profitability of the remote northwest stations.

In the early 1900s there was a golden five-year period when cattle were shipped from Wyndham to the Philippines for good prices. This market eventually collapsed, and once again the Kimberley cattle industry was in the doldrums. A small meatworks, established at Wyndham in 1919, provided a market for some Kimberley pastoralists, but this outlet was limited. The general Kimberley cattle prospect remained dim, and the situation did not improve, except for brief flushes, until the 1970s. By then the Durack empire had crumbled, and most of the pioneer families had disappeared from the northwest pastoral scene.

At the beginning of the 1970s, a new pattern of pastoral development emerged in the Kimberleys. Beef roads costing taxpayers $20 million were under construction. Australian, British and American development companies bought a number of grazing properties and spent further sums on improvement. A few individual American families did the same, migrating from cattle properties in the southern and mid-western parts of the United States.

Aboriginal dancer in a corroboree staged at the annual Boabab Festival, Derby

Malay crewman from a pearling lugger at Broome

West Kimberley aboriginal spear fisherman (W.A. government photo)

Horse-breakers saddle up on Leopold Downs station, west Kimberleys

Weather-smoothed rock outcrops near Port Hedland

Geikie Gorge, a tourist attraction near Fitzroy Crossing in the Kimberleys

Government building at Broome

Truck crossing the Sherlock River on the coastal highway near Whim Creek

Brahma bull at Yeeda station near Derby

An American cattleman in the Kimberley region. Large tracts of Kimberley grazing land is now American owned

Shearing time in the northwest. The area's wool production is small but a century of sheep grazing has caused serious degeneration of the landscape (W.A. government photo)

Cotton growing on the Ord has proved economically unsound but continues under subsidy

Irrigation farming experiments have been in progress at the Kimberley Research Farm for more than 20 years

New wharf at Broome makes shipping independent of massive northwest tides

A pearling lugger arrives at Broome after six weeks at sea

Essential liquid supplies (beer) coming ashore at Derby

Receding tide near Cable Beach at Broome. Sunbaking is more popular than swimming because of the shallowness and poisonous sea creatures

The modern, pleasant town of Kambalda juts like an island from a monotonous sea of vegetation

Coolgardie, a well-preserved ghost town, is a tourist-drawing museum of the west's golden era

Nickel miner underground at Kambalda (W.A. government photo)

The town of Mount Goldsworthy has not been designed to attract tourists (W.A. government photo)

Surveying at Mount Whaleback before mining commenced and the town of Newman was constructed (W.A. government photo)

In the open cut mine at Mount Tom-Price

Carnarvon from the air (W.A. government photo)

Sunset in the all-metal, pre-fabricated town of Newman near Mount Whaleback

Removing a hill to make way for the Port Hedland-Mount Whaleback railway

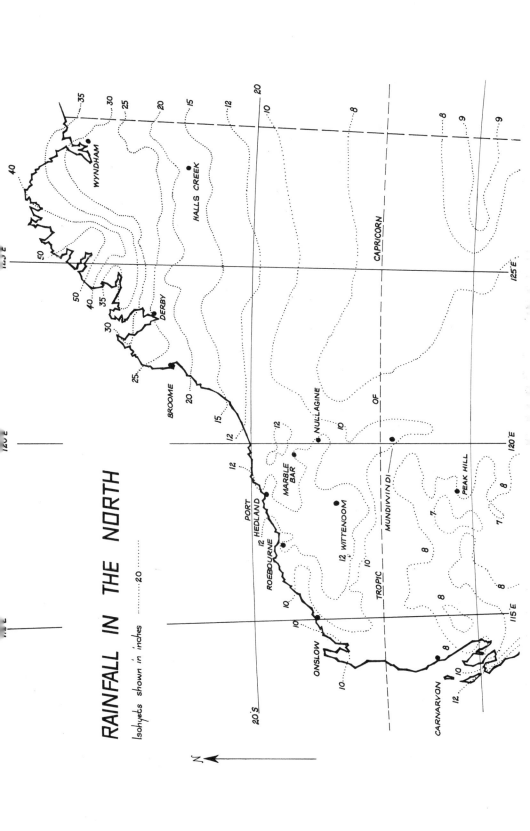

RAINFALL IN THE NORTH

Isohyets shown in inches .... 20 ....

N

The new owners provided themselves or their managers with comfortable air-conditioned homes — a basic requirement for any stable, tropical work force. Some properties were fenced into smaller blocks, so that stock could be properly managed. Herds were culled of poor quality "scrub" bulls, which were replaced with imported animals, some new breeds to the Kimberleys, such as Brahma and Santa Gertrudis. Cows were also culled, so that though stock numbers decreased temporarily, the retained herds were considerably better.

Improvement of Kimberley cattle stations has not been general. Many properties remain in the state of neglect and near dereliction that has been the rule, rather than the exception, in the northwest since the pioneering days. Whether improved markets can be found for the up-graded produce of the new-wave cattle stations remains to be seen. The large companies and wealthy individuals who have invested in the area — some with million-acre properties — seem confident.

In 1970, approximately 70% of all Kimberley cattle stations remained in the control of absentee-leaseholders. Only a handful of the properties are boundary fenced or have sufficient internal fencing to enable more than rudimentary grazing control. The open-range grazing system which has prevailed since the pioneer days has caused serious degeneration of the original Kimberley vegetation and near-disastrous erosion in wide areas.

Much of the watershed of the Ord Scheme has been described by northern cattle industry expert J. H. Kelly as "the worst eroded lands of northern Australia — probably of any part of Australia"! The erosion is a direct result of gross over-stocking for long periods.

Continued erosion in the watershed areas could ultimately clog the entire Ord Irrigation Scheme, which will cost the Australian taxpayer more than $100 million to complete. Most of the eroding watershed land is leased by one oversea pastoral company, which controls 5 million acres in the Kimberley region. (The legal maximum area for one owner is 1 million acres, though this law was under review in 1970.) For this land, the company pays a yearly rent of round $2 a 1,000 acres. The company's leases were extended in 1965 to the year 2015.

The Western Australian Government spent $5 million between 1960 and 1965, trying to reafforest the eroded land, which one Member of Parliament described as being "as bare as bitumen". The company was asked to pay $160,000 towards this land reclamation scheme, on the understanding that the area would be handed back to it eventually for further exploitation when vegetation was sufficiently regrown.

The method used to regenerate this eroded area included contouring and extensive sowing of buffel and birdwood grass, and kapok bush. The area was fenced to keep stock out. More than 25,000 donkeys, found running wild, were destroyed. To date, regeneration has been slow, though a further $60,000 has been spent yearly on the project since 1965.

The company may have to wait some time before its cattle are permitted back in this vital watershed area. However, this would once again place the entire Ord Scheme in jeopardy.

Cattle grazing on a limited scale has been practised in other regions of the northwest since the earliest days of settlement. Between the Murchison and De Grey rivers, inland to Nullagine and Wiluna, in what is basically sheep and mining territory, approximately 65,000 head of cattle are grazed.

This is a small number when compared with the Kimberley cattle population of 550,000, the Western Australia State total of 1.3 million and the national total of 19 million cattle.

Agriculture and the Ord Scheme

In 1872, speaking of the future of agriculture in the northwest, Governor Sir Frederick Weld said: *Looking upon the country geologically it at once becomes evident that it is only now in the course of that process of transformation which will fully prepare it for the occupation of man. Piled-up masses of rock, split and rent by the action of tropical suns and showers . . . are resolved by degrees into heaps of broken stones of all shapes and sizes; they again are further reduced by the same process to shingle or gravel then to the fine red dust which is caught by the tufty spinifex and forms plains and valleys of rich soil, only wanting an admixture of decayed vegetable matter and irrigation to be ready to grow the most lavish wealth of tropical produce.*

History has not vindicated the extraordinary optimism of Governor Weld, who failed to explain where the decayed vegetable matter and irrigation water would come from. With the exception of the Geraldton wheat lands and Carnarvon's banana and vegetable farms, no part of the New Frontier has yet produced any profitable crops of national significance.

Explorer Frank Gregory claimed in 1861 to have found 200,000 acres of land suitable for cotton and other crops on the deltas of the De Grey and other rivers. His optimistic report led to nothing. The country round Port Hedland and south to Dampier which so inspired Gregory remains to this day almost devoid of agriculture. The spinifex and rock still await time's alchemy to transmute them into fertile soil. Governor Weld's dream of miraculous irrigation waters remains unfulfilled.

A new dream of agricultural splendour in the northwest gained popularity in the mid-twentieth century, and was partly realized during the 1960s in the Ord River Scheme. In the 70s the Scheme seems destined to grow considerably, though its future productivity and profitability are doubted by some experts. The mantle of optimism under which the Ord Scheme has developed is maintained by the Western Australian Government. By 1970, more than $20 million was spent on the project, and a $70 million expansion programme is now in progress.

Some agricultural scientists and economists, among them Doctor Bruce Davidson, have persistently criticized the Ord Scheme and predicted its ultimate failure as an economically viable agricultural scheme Doctor Davidson is a distinguished Australian

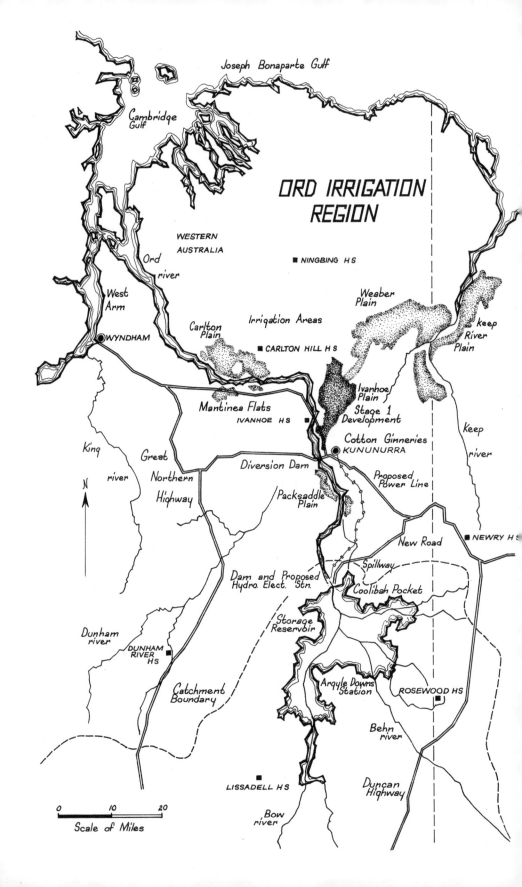

agricultural scientist and economist, internationally known for his research into land use in Britain and Africa.

To date, most of Doctor Davidson's criticisms have been vindicated. The Ord's main crop, cotton, has proved a failure. Cotton growing continues under government subsidy, but Ord production costs are above world cotton prices and prospects remain dim. Other Ord crops remain in the pilot stage.

The first Kimberley experimental crops were grown in the late 1940s. It is significant that after 30 years, only one crop, cotton, has so far been attempted on a sizeable commercial scale — and this has failed.

Other crops such as sugar, which grows well in the Kimberleys, have not been attempted commercially because of the continuing world surplus of sugar. Weeds and insect pests, which thrive in the humid tropical Kimberley conditions, present a growing threat to the Ord irrigation crops. Constant aerial spraying has proved necessary, with resultant pollution of the adjacent Timor Sea.

Sorghum and other fodder crops may eventually be the major produce of the Ord Scheme. American, British and some Australian development companies have invested heavily in surrounding cattle-grazing properties. They think that in the years to come the expanded Ord Scheme will provide an economic source of cattle fodder.

This seems probable. All previous experience indicates that cotton, sugar, rice, safflower and other crops cannot be grown economically. Perhaps the expanding Ord Scheme is really intended as a source of stock fodder for the Kimberley cattle stations.

Wheat growing in the Geraldton district, on the southern border of the New Frontier, represents the only large-scale form of agriculture practised in the northwest. The port exports round 20 million bushels of grain yearly. Plans were made for an increase to 30 million bushels in the 1970s but Australia was over-producing wheat in 1969-70, and quotas were introduced to limit rather than expand production. With a national wheat surplus, Geraldton's grain expansion plans may have to be shelved.

Although geographically outside the scope of this book, the new agricultural lands near Esperance deserve mention because of the New Frontier atmosphere of this burgeoning district. Previously regarded as unsuitable for agriculture, 2.5 million acres of sandy heath plain is rapidly changing into farmland. Another four million acres of adjacent mallee-type scrub may also be cleared for agriculture. Development followed work carried out by a Western Australian Department of Agriculture research farm, established in 1949. Scientists found that trace elements, superphosphate and legume crops made the "hungry" soil fertile.

An early attempt by American financier Allen T. Chase to develop 1.5 million acres for resale failed, but since then, 600 farms have been established. The 2.5 million-acre region now runs over one million sheep and approximately 40,000 cattle. Wheat production from 110,000 acres in 1969 was 1.5 million bushels. Expansion of the

Esperance wheatlands was planned, but the persisting national surplus of this grain may force developers and farmers to reconsider the project.

Development costs for Esperance land have ranged from $25 to $50 an acre. Land developed for $50 (and in some cases more), is in the hands of American millionaires such as David Rockefeller, Art Linkletter and Benno Schmidt. Development costs of this magnitude are well beyond the resources of ordinary settlers using borrowed capital. The major returns from such inflated development costs come as tax reductions on income derived elsewhere by the millionaires concerned.

The small number of eye-catching over-capitalized American-owned properties have been greatly publicized, imparting a rather unwarranted glamour to the Esperance region.

In the same area, Australians who have borrowed up to $50,000 to develop their 2,000 acre properties live with their families in machinery and shearing sheds because they can't afford a house. Those with homes have incurred even larger debts. Annual loan repayments and interest charges can swallow half the farmer's net income.

The situation round Esperance is not unlike that of Victoria's Mallee and the adjoining country in South Australia, some years ago. Similar land was cleared by large organizations, for resale as subdivided wheat and wool properties. Trace elements were used to make sandy soils productive. Subsequent erosion, decreasing soil fertility, bad seasons and interest charges forced many farmers to offer their properties for sale.

Only future events will reveal if there is an overall similarity in the pattern of development of the Mallee and Esperance projects.

Fishing and pearling
The State of Western Australia has Australia's wealthiest fishery and the near-north coast produces the richest harvests. The Geraldton area's annual lobster catch is worth more than N.S.W.'s entire fish production. Each year, Western Australia sends $19 million worth of crayfish tails to America — N.S.W.'s total fish catch is worth only $12 million by comparison. In addition to the crayfish, fishermen on the New Frontier also catch $3 million worth of prawns and scale fish, while pearl farming in the far north fetches another $3 million yearly.

Although prospects in the 1970s are excellent the New Frontier's fishing industry could fail, as it has on previous occasions. Pearling, once the northwest's glamour fishery, collapsed last century and has never recovered. Where once there were 400 pearling boats there are now ten.

More recently, a crayfishing boom in northern waters fizzled out to nothing. Production reached a peak of 290,000 pounds in 1961, dropped to 8,500 pounds in 1964 and was nil in 1965. Over-fishing was the apparent cause.

In 1970, the total catch of crayfish was round 19 million pounds, representing Australia's biggest fishery. Most of the shellfish come from the Geraldton area and waters to the south. Whether this enormous production can be maintained is unknown. The spectacular failure of the northern crayfishing industry should stand as a warning to the southern fishery.

Without its annual $19 million crayfish bonanza, Western Australia's fishery is small compared with other Australian States.

Two other New Frontier fisheries could expand considerably in the 1970s. Surveys indicate that prawning off the Pilbara coast between Onslow and Port Hedland may be profitable. But the future of this fishery is uncertain — since likely pollution from the new iron ports could have an adverse effect. Farther north, surveys by the Western Australian Department of Fisheries and Fauna have indicated commercial quantities of prawns between Admiralty Gulf and Cape Londonderry. Scallop fishing in the Carnarvon area may have commercial possibilities and shark fishing, for export to Germany, is also being studied.

Tuna fishing, already in the pioneering stages in southern waters of Western Australia, could have a big future off the coasts of the New Frontier. Large schools of blue and yellow-fin tuna are sighted regularly all along the northwest coast to the Timor Sea, north of Wyndham.

Japanese boats have been tuna fishing 100 to 200 miles off the northwest coast for some time, averaging 45,000 tons yearly. This quantity of tuna is worth $22.5 million on the international market. Russian ships, up to 10,000 tons, also fish the ocean west of the New Frontier. They plan to use freezer-trawlers up to 40,000 tons. West German fishing organizations are known to be interested in the same area.

The existing off-shore foreign fishery and local surveys of territorial waters indicate good tuna-fishing possibilities. But large boats and mainland factories or factory ships will be needed for economic development, according to the Western Australian Department of Fisheries and Fauna.

Australians have been traditionally cautious of investing large sums in fishing ventures. Michael Kailis, the New Frontier's prawning and crayfish "king", is among the most likely future tuna fishermen. The British-owned firm of Ross Fisheries is also interested in tuna fishing.

The Kailis family of fishermen present a classic New Frontier tale of rags-to-riches. George Kailis was a Greek fisherman who migrated to northern Australia in the 1920s. For a time he was a diver in Darwin, a cane-cutter in Queensland and a railway-sleeper cutter, in southern Western Australia. Then he moved to Perth and began a suburban fish peddling business, tramping the streets with a horse and cart. That was in 1927.

Years later, helped by his sons Theo and Michael, he built up a crayfish processing business worth $400,000. The family sold out to the British company Ross Fisheries, the world's largest fish catching and processing organization. Theo Kailis became managing director of the new Australian branch of Ross Fisheries.

Michael Kailis attended university with the intention of following a professional career — but fishing was in his blood. Today he operates Gulf Fisheries, a prawning and crayfishing enterprise second only to the Ross group. The company has its own

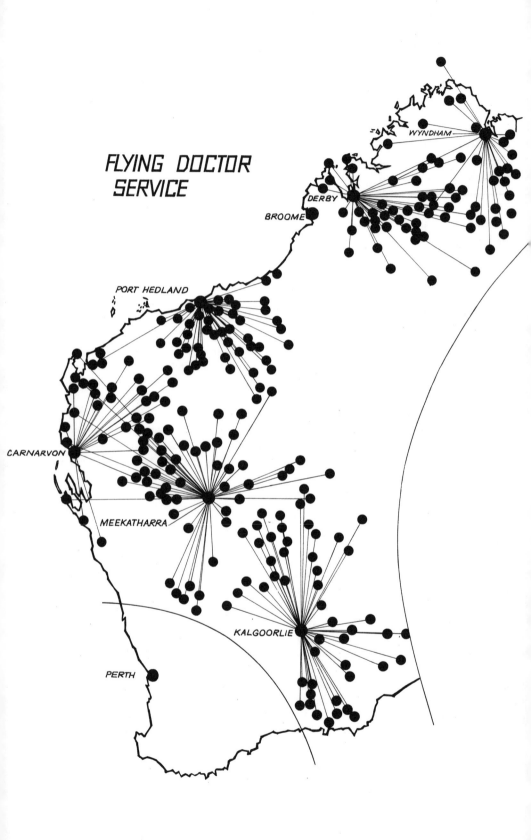

FLYING DOCTOR
SERVICE

WYNDHAM

DERBY
BROOME

PORT HEDLAND

CARNARVON

MEEKATHARRA

KALGOORLIE

PERTH

fleet of crayfishing and prawning boats and at times buys the catches of independent fishermen to supply its processing plants at Dongara, Exmouth and Groote Eylandt. (The last-mentioned factory, in the Northern Territory, is staffed by aboriginal workers, mainly women, and supplied by aboriginal fishermen.)

Michael Kailis, a vigorous, straight-talking, down-to-earth man with twinkling eyes and sun-browned skin, is reputedly a millionaire. He is at times seen in the slick offices of Gulf Fisheries in Perth. But he prefers to spend much of his time in shorts and bare feet aboard his fishing boats, scattered round the coast from Geraldton to the Gulf of Carpentaria. At such times, in appearance and manner, he is indistinguishable from the wild assortment of colourful personalities who crew his and other New Frontier fishing boats.

The trade seems to attract characters from all parts of the world. In the Abrolhos, one island is called Basili — after a large Sicilian migrant family who have made it their headquarters. Family patriarch, Papa Basili, sports a gay Sicilian cummerbund and fishes mostly at night with a strong light over the boat's prow to attract fish.

Geraldton, not an easy port in which to gain notice, boasts one of Australia's few licensed professional fisherwomen, Miss Muriel Thomas. (Another was Mrs Eva Warren, of Eden, N.S.W.) Miss Thomas used to be a professional fisherwoman on the famous Dogger Bank cod grounds in the North Sea.

Pearling in the northwest was pioneered by Pemberton Walcott at Cossack in the late 1860s. He and other settlers noticed that local Aborigines wore necklaces of mother-of-pearl, made from shells they picked up along the beaches. It became a practice for settlers to go beach-combing for pearl shell, in the slack season on their sheep properties.

When all the easy shell had been picked up, they employed the Aborigines to "bob-under" in shallow water for the shell. Later the Aborigines dived from small boats, to depths of five fathoms. By 1868, there was a rush for pearl shell in the district, after the manner of the later gold-rushes. The first specially constructed pearling boat was built by Charles Harper for his own use around Cossack. By 1874, local production of pearl shell and pearls was worth $160,000 yearly (more than the annual district wool-clip). Value of the pearls was $25,000.

In the heyday of Cossack's pearling era, the late 1870s, some 76 luggers operated from the port. An old identity, W. A. Thompson, recalls: *I have been astonished to learn from visitors that they have been informed that the Japanese were the main owners pearling here in the old days. On the contrary, the Japanese had least interest in the industry. Of the Asiatics at either Cossack or Roebourne, the Japanese were a minority, except for Japanese women ... Very few Japanese were employed in operating the pearling fleet from Cossack. The majority of those working the luggers were Malays and Manila men, in the employ of European owners. They would control and supply from a schooner, always known as the Mother Ship. The mother ships would control possibly five to ten luggers each. The luggers would start dribbling in* towards the end of September and the last would probably have arrived by end of November and the mother ships following.

The luggers needing repairs to under-water copper sheathings, deck caulking, or any other work, would lay up at the western end of the township on a beautiful wide sandy beach, which was a feature of Cossack's foreshore up to the year 1900; but seems to have deteriorated since then, by the extensive collection of mud and mangrove growth at both western and eastern ends of the old port.

The remainder of the luggers would anchor securely in the protected waters, in lee of the mangrove island, lying one third the length of Cossack creek at the western end . . . The lay-up of the fleet each year caused a big increase in the population of Chinatown from a normal 120 to approximately 350. This increase usually led to sundry brawls, stabbings, or as on one occasion, shooting . . . Trouble at Chinatown often broke out whilst the Chinese celebrated their annual festive occasion, the main feature of which was a huge moving dragon. On one such occasion our leading Cossack Chinese storekeeper had his throat cut at Roebourne Chinatown.

Thompson also recollected several of the cyclones that occasionally ravaged the pearling coast: Cyclones, or as we knew them, Willy Willies were a problem to be reckoned with. All houses, including stone built or otherwise, had their roofs anchored to the earth by heavy wire rigging as used by the larger vessels . . . The only two blows I can recall from personal experience was 1894 and 1898.

During the first half of the '94 blow the lighter Cossack came over the road, struck the corner verandah post of our house and passed on to the rear, finishing up against the back road along with all other wreckage gathered up by the flood waters. A lull of 15 to 20 minutes then ensued, after which interval the wind came back from the opposite direction.

In the meantime the water had risen above our floor boards and about six milking goats which had sought refuge underneath the house were drowned . . . During the lull it was observed that the pearling mother schooner Harriet was lying in front of the house . . . Another schooner was on dry land at the eastern side of the jetty and several luggers were sunk or dismantled (one crew member was drowned at the anchorage) and others driven across the marsh. This was the same blow that caused the sinking of the schooner Ann in the foam passage, with the tragic death of the Erickson family and others, and when our school house was also destroyed.

The next serious blow occurred in 1898. At its warning we all shifted to the billiard room on the lee side of Brett's house, near Nanny Goat Hill, which was occupied at the time by Malachy Meagher and his young bride just recently up from the south. Their wedding presents were laid out on the billiard table and a grand piano stood in one corner. Very shortly after the blow started, the roof lifted off and we had to enter the main building via a rear door. Things were going badly with Mr Meagher, as his front window was caving in, despite heavy shutters. The property was saved by quickly bolstering the windows with double bed and mattress. Another couple who had their

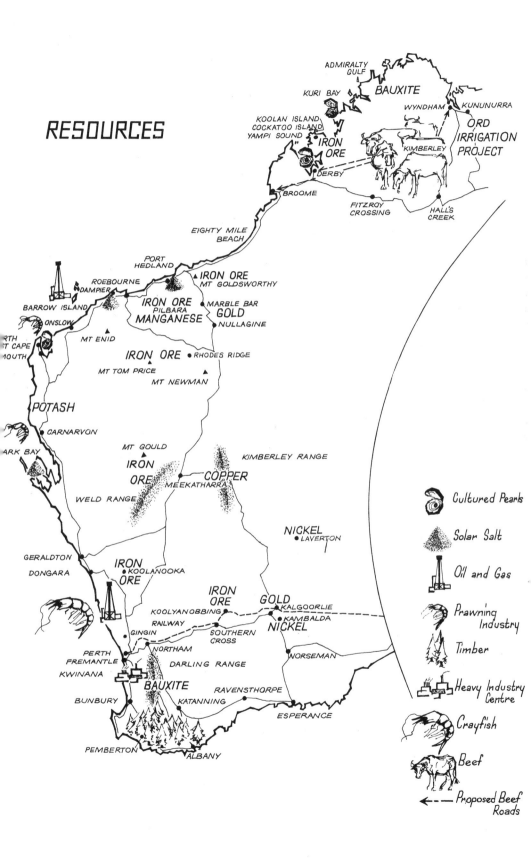

RESOURCES

ADMIRALTY GULF

KURI BAY

BAUXITE

KOOLAN ISLAND
COCKATOO ISLAND
YAMPI SOUND

WYNDHAM

KUNUNURRA

IRON ORE

ORD IRRIGATION PROJECT

KIMBERLEY

DERBY

BROOME

FITZROY CROSSING

HALL'S CREEK

EIGHTY MILE BEACH

PORT HEDLAND

ROEBOURNE

DAMPIER

IRON ORE ▲ MT GOLDSWORTHY

BARROW ISLAND

ONSLOW

IRON ORE
PILBARA
MANGANESE

MARBLE BAR

GOLD

NULLAGINE

MT ENID

IRON ORE • RHODES RIDGE

RTH
T CAPE
OUTH

MT TOM PRICE

MT NEWMAN

POTASH

CARNARVON

MT GOULD

KIMBERLEY RANGE

IRON ORE

COPPER

ARK BAY

MEEKATHARRA

WELD RANGE

NICKEL
• LAVERTON

GERALDTON

DONGARA

IRON ORE
• KOOLANOOKA

IRON ORE

GOLD

KALGOORLIE

KOOLYANOBBING

RAILWAY

SOUTHERN CROSS

KAMBALDA

NICKEL

GINGIN

PERTH
FREMANTLE

NORTHAM

DARLING RANGE

NORSEMAN

KWINANA

BAUXITE

RAVENSTHORPE

BUNBURY

KATANNING

ESPERANCE

PEMBERTON

ALBANY

Cultured Pearls

Solar Salt

Oil and Gas

Prawning Industry

Timber

Heavy Industry Centre

Crayfish

Beef

← --- Proposed Beef Roads

roof lifted tried to make their way to the new school near by and as soon as hit by the wind, they were parted and hung on behind separate clumps of coastal spinifex (not the prickly kind). Neither party knew what had become of the other until the storm was over.

Luggers were sunk and small vessels wrecked in the creek. The SS Beagle had broken from her moorings at the jetty, swung round on to the rocks and finished up with her stern almost on the tram station platform . . . SS Croydon had been tied up in the shelter of the Deep Hole jetty, but she broke away and finished up on dry land well above highwater mark.

In 1880, the price of pearl shell dropped sharply. Prices improved during the 1890s, but the supply of shell accessible to skin-divers was seriously depleted. Cossack's brief light flickered out.

In the period of Cossack's decline, new pearl-beds were discovered farther north. Luggers began working out of Broome, officially declared a town in 1883. Shell, some containing pearls, had been picked up along the district beaches since the first attempt at settlement in 1864. One of the world's most famous pearls, the Southern Cross, now in the Vatican Collection and valued at $48,000, was reputedly found by a boy playing on a beach near Broome.

The main lure of pearling in the early days was the great value of the pearls. Shell was a saleable product, but of secondary importance. As pearls became scarcer, the shell assumed major importance. The pattern was similar to that at Cossack: the shell beds readily accessible to skin divers were fished out and the industry languished until the introduction, in the early 1900s, of the diving suit opened up new, deeper waters.

By 1925, Broome reached its peak as a pearling centre with a population of about five thousand. There were 400 boats operating out of the port, employing 3,000 men, chiefly Asians — the most common being Malays, Japanese, Manilamen, Koepangers and Chinese.

The large fleet soon fished out the shallower oyster-beds and by the beginning of World War II, most diving was at depths of 15 to 20 fathoms. The industry lapsed in the war and, largely through competition from plastic materials, has not recovered.

Another cause of the persisting depression in the industry was the entry into Australian territorial waters of pearling fleets from other nations, particularly Japan. This caused an oversupply of pearl-shell and a subsequent drop in prices. Australian pearl-shell is of high quality, but needs a controlled market to hold its value.

In the post-war period, the average annual harvest by the surviving ten luggers fishing out of Broome has been $150,000. Of this amount about $10,000 yearly has come from pearls, the rest from shell. The Broome luggers are owned by an Australian firm headed by Kimberley Male, whose family co-founded the historic northwest company of Streeter and Male. The boats are crewed chiefly by Malays, some from Kuala Lumpur, others from Singapore, and the diver on each boat is usually Japanese.

The boats have a crew of nine and generally stay out on the oyster-beds for six weeks to harvest between 10 and 12 tons of shell.

The development of the pearl culture industry in northern Australian waters during the 1960s has given a fillip to the Broome pearlers. Pearl culture was pioneered here in 1956 by Japanese pearl farmer Hiro Awaki, with American and Australian backing.

Today, there are three organizations growing cultured pearls along the northwest coast. They are Alf Morgan and Son at Exmouth Gulf, Dean Brown and Son at Cape Leveque and W.A. Pearls Limited, at Kuri Bay. The Broome luggers sell live oysters in their shells to the pearl farmers for $2,000 a ton. The Kuri Bay company alone buys $110,000 worth of shell yearly.

To stimulate the growth of a pearl, tiny beads of irritant material are placed in the oyster's flesh. The oyster secretes nacre, the substance which lines its shell, round the bead to form a pearl. Extreme skill is required to position the bead, wrapped in a piece of oyster mantle tissue, so that a complete pearl will form. A mistake can kill the oyster.

Half pearls can be induced to grow artificially where the mother-of-pearl is laid down inside the oyster shell. These are marketable, but are of insignificant value when compared with spherical pearls, which sell for as much as $3,000 each. Cultured pearl oysters are suspended in baskets hanging from anchored rafts in shallow bay waters. For success in pearl farming, there must be an ideal combination of water temperature, food materials, currents and freedom from parasites and storm disturbance.

Australian production of cultured pearls now exceeds one ton yearly; Japan produces 50 tons. Local pearls mature in two years, but in Japan the process takes four years. Australian pearl production was valued at $3 million in 1970.

Whaling in northwestern waters was pioneered by the Norwegian Whaling Company at Point Cloates, near Carnarvon, in 1912. (Whales were taken occasionally in the 1870s, but there was no industry of any significance until the Norwegians commenced operations.)

In 1921, an Australian whaling company was formed, but it fished for only two seasons. The Norwegians had meanwhile departed, to return in 1925-8, when they processed about 3,500 whales, mostly humpbacks. After that, there was no mainland-based whaling industry, though whales were taken in Western Australian waters by foreign deep-sea boats throughout the 1930s.

In 1949, northwest whaling was re-established at Point Cloates and near-by Babbage Island. Production reached $2 million yearly until the International Whaling Commission completely protected humpback whales in 1963; the industry lapsed. (Whales had already been hunted to extinction in the northern hemisphere and it was hoped to prevent repetition of this disaster in southern waters.)

The pattern of most forms of northwest fishing has been one of marked changes of fortune, with frequent downward plunges to extinction after brief boom periods.

Culture pearl farming and lobster fishing are now rapidly developing, and it is hoped that this boom can be sustained.

Marketing solar salt
The New Frontier's solar salt industry reflects the pattern of the northwest's entire mineral industry: Japan needs four million tons of salt annually; Western Australia has the salt; American firms are collecting and selling the salt to Japan.

The salt is not used as a table product, but is required by the Japanese chemical industry (more than 90% of the world's salt production is used for industrial purposes). Japan's present salt needs are expected to grow steadily. Mexico previously supplied Japan with salt, but northwest Australia has proved a cheaper source of supply of this commodity — as well as iron ore, which Japan also used to buy at a higher price from South America.

The Leslie Salt Company of America has established the world's second largest solar salt plant at Port Hedland and is now supplying one million tons annually to Japan. Output will rise to 2.5 million tons in the 1970s.

The salt is obtained by pumping water from the near-by Indian Ocean on to 52,000 acres of low-lying drying pans where it is left for six months to dry in the sun. The hard salt is then heaped up into stock piles, brine-washed, drained and taken by road-train about six miles to Port Hedland's export wharves.

Another solar-salt venture in Shark Bay, near Carnarvon, is shipping salt to Japan. Production is expected to reach 1.5 million tons annually in the 1970s.

A Japanese-Australian project at Dampier began shipping salt to Japan in 1970, with a proposed annual target of one million tons. Salt is also produced at Exmouth Gulf and at Lake Lefroy, adjacent to the nickel mining town of Kambalda.

Further potential salt-producing areas are being examined — and it seems only a matter of time before a mining company discovers Lake Eyre's 3,000 square miles of already dried, rock-hard salt.

A Canadian company, Texada Mines Limited, plans to extract potash from 800-square-mile Lake McLeod, near Carnarvon. Production is estimated at 240,000 tons yearly, which would more than supply Australia's current demands for this fertilizer.

Mining boom

Government proclamations clearly establish that all minerals in and under the soil of Australia belong to the Crown, represented by the various State governments. No private individual or company can claim any oil, gold, coal or other minerals beneath land it owns, leases or rents. Prospective miners must apply for permission to commence mining; and pay a royalty to the Government for any mineral dug out. A miner must also sell all the gold he produces to the Crown, at the ruling government-controlled price.

If the mineral is discovered on "private" property and the Government considers it in the public interest to extract the mineral, the owner or occupier of the land may be required to vacate his property. Compensation is paid for the land at the current market value. The value of the minerals beneath the land is not considered, for the individual has no rights to these.

The Crown hold ownership of the minerals on behalf of the people of Australia and their elected Governments. So the people collectively own the mineral wealth of the nation. Every man, woman and child in Australia, as the law now stands, is a part-owner in the raw materials of the current mineral bonanza.

In the early days

Mining on the New Frontier has a long history. Thomas Mason discovered copper in 1842 at Wanerenooka, and the exploring Gregory brothers found lead on the Murchison River north of Geraldton, in 1848. By the end of that year, the Geraldine Mine was functioning and was visited by the Governor of Western Australia, Charles Fitzgerald. Deposits of lead and copper were found at Northampton, between the Geraldine Mine and Geraldton, in 1848. This led to the construction of the colony's first railway, from Northampton to Geraldton, in 1879.

Guano was mined on islands near Shark Bay in 1850.

The first goldfield in the colony was officially proclaimed in 1886, in the Kimberley district, near the town of Hall's Creek. In 1883, John Forrest (then surveyor-general of the colony) and government geologist E. T. Hardman, reported that the Kimberley might contain gold. Adam Johns and Philip Saunders had already found some "colour" in the upper Margaret and Ord rivers. Charles Hall and John Slattery discovered alluvial gold in 1885. Their find was not a big one, but a rush developed, largely as a result of exaggerated stories told by local characters such as William Carr Boyd. He had been a surveyor for the Cambridge Downs Pastoral Association which planned to graze sheep on the lower Ord River in the Kimberley.

Gold mining was established in the Nullagine area south of Marble Bar in 1887-8, following discoveries by Roebourne pastoralists Withnell, Cooke, Lorden and Wells. A settlement grew up at Marble Bar, which became the centre of the Pilbara goldfield. A railway linked the town with Port Hedland in 1912.

In 1889, discovery of gold along the Ashburton River started another rush. A total 20,000 ounces of gold was found on the Pilbara and Ashburton fields during their initial boom periods; but later finds were of little significance.

The opening of the Coolgardie and Kalgoorlie goldfields in the early 1890s eclipsed all other mining booms in the colony of Western Australia. For more than 60 years after Federation, no other mineral strike in Western Australia matched the gleaming bonanza of Paddy Hannan's field.

Smaller strikes of gold were made at Southern Cross, Mount Magnet, Wiluna, Laverton and other places; but none rivalled Kalgoorlie's wealth. Copper and tin were mined from Peak Hill to Port Hedland, on a small scale, by individual miners or small companies and partnerships. Copper (57 tons) was first mined in the Bowes and Murchison districts, in 1856; and alluvial tin found at Cooglegoon Creek, 45 miles southwest of Marble Bar.

Asbestos was discovered in the Hamersley Range in 1917, but mining was considered uneconomic in such a remote area. A report by government mineralogist E. S. Simpson, in 1929, briefly rekindled interest in asbestos mining, following evaluation of asbestos specimens from Mount Margaret and Weeli Wolli Creek — sites west and east of Wittenoom Gorge. Some asbestos mining took place in 1937-8 at Lionel, and a mine was established at Yampire Gorge in 1939. The first major asbestos mining venture commenced operations in 1943 at Wittenoom Gorge, where a subsidiary of the Colonial Sugar Refining Company extracted blue asbestos.

After the compass difficulties experienced by Frank Gregory and other explorers and settlers in the northwest, geologists surveyed extensive iron ore fields in the 1890s, between the Murchison and Gascoyne rivers.

In 1895, government geologist Harry P. Woodward, writing of the northwest corner of the colony, mentioned ... *immense lodes, and would be of enormous value if cheap labour were abundant, there would be enough to supply the whole world should the present sources be worked out ... This is essentially an iron country, it being impossible to travel even a short distance without encountering a deposit or lode, owing to which it is almost impossible to work a magnetic compass with any degree of accuracy.*

A traveller enjoys a drink from the Paddy Hannan memorial fountain in
Kalgoorlie

Twilight on the corner of Hannan and Maritana streets, in the business hub of Kalgoorlie. The district nickel rush, triggered by the Poseidon company's finds in 1969, has revitalized the large but previously ailing gola city

Although a ghost town, Coolgardie has a bright future as a tourist attraction. Its substantial buildings are being refurbished to make the whole town a museum of the golden era

Nostalgia on a window in Kalgoorlie's main street

BAYLEY STREET

OH! MEN HAVE COME AND MEN HAVE GONE
SINCE BAYLEY'S STAR GLEAMED BRIGHT
AND NEW LIGHTS SHINE WHERE OLD LIGHTS SHONE
IN BAYLEY STREET TONIGHT.

AND DID YOU SEE THOSE GRAND OLD MEN
BRIGHT-EYED THOUGH BOWED AND GREY,
RETURNING TO THE 'FIELDS AGAIN
LIKE GHOSTS OF YESTERDAY?

THE HUMAN TIDE SWEPT SWIFTLY WEST
THEN SLOWLY EBBED AGAIN,
AND SOME FULFILLED THEIR GOLDEN QUEST
AND SOME FOUND LOSS AND PAIN.

AND SOME RETURNED TO WHENCE THEY CAME
WITH WEALTH AND TALES TO TELL,
AND SOME FOUND GRAVES THAT BEAR NO NAM
AND SOME STILL WITH US DWELL.

NOW FORTY YEARS HAVE PASSED AWAY
(TWELVE THOUSAND SUNS HAVE SET);
AND FROM THAT ROARING YESTERDAY,
THE ECHOES LINGER YET.

JACK SORENSON

*Mineral claims flutter on notice boards outside government offices in
Hannan Street, Kalgoorlie*

*Main street of Norseman, the first town of any size that travellers across
the Nullarbor encounter after leaving Ceduna in South Australia*

Burt Street in Boulder, the town that is Kalgoorlie's Siamese-twin. Though physically attached to each other the towns maintain their separate identities. Kalgoorlie is the major commercial shopping and business centre, but most of the district mines are in Boulder

The mine at Tom Price. Despite many stories to the contrary, open cut mining of this type requires only modest technical know-how. Without any imported expertise, Australia could have easily mined the Pilbara ore deposits, using borrowed money just as the American and other foreign mining companies have done (W.A. government photo)

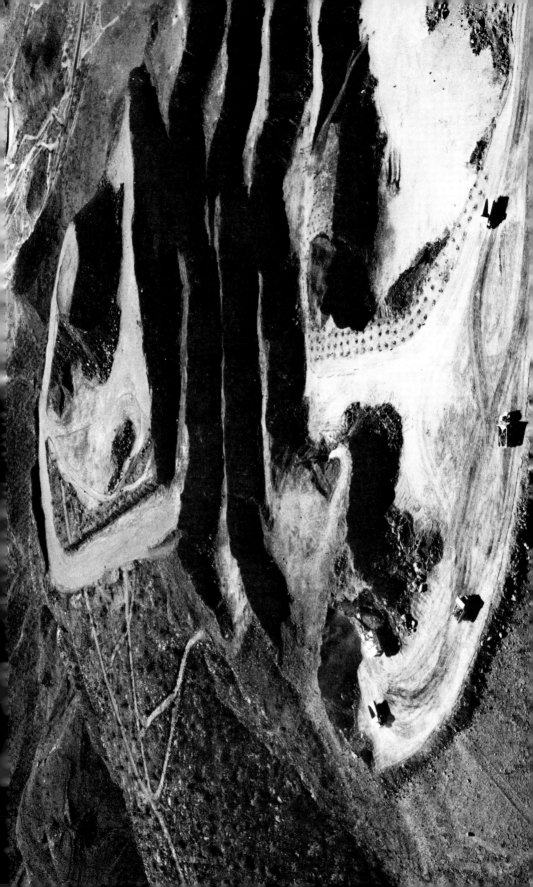

The ore train line from the port of Dampier to Mount Tom Price. It was built quickly and cheaply by Torres Strait islanders when the "Kanaka trade" was briefly revived in the mid-1960s

A huge mobile shovel gouging out ore at Tom Price to load into 100-ton capacity trucks (C.R.A. photo)

Hard-hatted travellers on a company bus tour of an ore town

Signing the original Tom Price ore contract in Tokyo (C.R.A. photo)

Strollers in the small but modern shopping centre at Tom Price

American company representatives look over a map of their Pilbara holdings (C.R.A. photo)

Not all the New Frontier's mineral riches are red in colour. Rare white quartz for use in tile manufacture on its way to the Meekatharra railhead

The Port Hedland-Mount Waleback ore railway under construction. The 265-mile line opened in 1969 (B.H.P. photo)

Early days on the Mount Newman and Mount Whaleback project. Large quantities of ore are now being exported via Port Hedland to Japan. Two Australian companies, Colonial Sugar Refining and Broken Hill Proprietary, have sizeable interests in the Newman-Whaleback venture (B.H.P. photo)

An ore train from Mount Whaleback on its way to Port Hedland. The American-Australian partnership at Mount Whaleback is called the Mount Newman Mining Company and the name of the company town near the mine site is Newman. The company also has its own new suburb in Port Hedland called Cooke Point (B.H.P. photo)

An oilwell pump in operation on Barrow Island. Gas from the field drives the pump motor (WAPET photo)

Roughnecks on the drilling floor of a rig on Barrow Island (WAPET photo)

The Western Australian Year Book of 1902 records: *The iron ore deposits of the Murchison area ... though neglected at present are destined to form a very important state asset ... In the Weld Range is said to be one of the richest iron lodes in the world.* This was estimated to be round 27 million tons.

By 1917, only 100 tons of iron ore, worth $600, had been mined in the northwest, at Whim Creek. (In the south, 57,000 tons of iron ore, worth $140,000, had been mined in the Darling Ranges.)

By 1932, government mineralogist E. S. Simpson recorded: *Deposits of iron are very plentiful in Western Australia, many of them obviously containing many millions of tons of ore readily obtainable by quarrying and open-cut mining ... They have had little attention given to them up to the present as sources of metallic iron, as conditions are adverse to trading such low-priced material to distant markets ... With progress in time, however, these potential sources of wealth will doubtless be utilised ...*

Great ore bodies of haematite are found close to the coast at Yampi Sound, and near Roebourne .... from which ore could be very readily placed upon ocean-going vessels for export to the world's markets.

Simpson's prophecy of 1932, particularly concerning the Pilbara iron ore deposits, has proved remarkably accurate. His prediction concerning Yampi Sound came true in 1951 — when the Australian firm of Broken Hill Proprietary Limited began shipping ore to its steelworks at Port Kembla in N.S.W. The Hoskins Iron and Steel Company (now part of the B.H.P. complex) acquired mineral leases on Cockatoo Island, near Yampi Sound, as early as 1927.

Despite the great distance from Yampi Sound to Port Kembla, the project was very profitable. The major cost, transport, was kept low through the use of company-owned ships. A royalty of 15 cents a ton was paid for the ore. Yampi Sound and near-by Cockatoo Island still provide raw material for the Port Kembla steel-making complex.

Although the Government of Western Australia and the Commonwealth Government knew about the ore bodies in the Pilbara, they considered them to be of poor quality and didn't bother to prove their exact extent. Proving a mineral deposit involves extensive drilling — a costly project the Governments did not embark on. The world was (and is) over-supplied with iron ore, and there seemed no likelihood of oversea markets for the "low grade" ore known to exist in northwest Australia.

Until 1960, the official government figure for all proved iron ore deposits in Australia was less than 500 million tons. Export of raw iron ore was prohibited. The prohibition gave rise to a popular misconception that Australia's only known iron ore deposits were those already being mined, at places such as Yampi Sound and Iron Knob (South Australia).

As Simpson in 1932, and others before him, had documented the huge Pilbara and Murchison deposits of "low grade" ore, the popular notion that Australia was deficient in iron had little foundation. In 1959, Dr J. A. Dunn, chief mineral economist of the

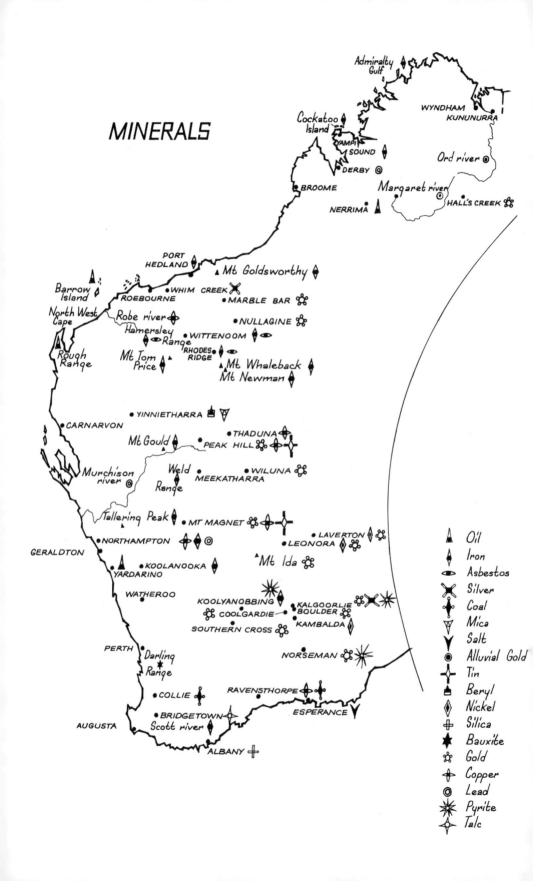

MINERALS

Admiralty Gulf
WYNDHAM
KUNUNURRA
Cockatoo Island
YAMPI SOUND
Ord river
DERBY
BROOME
Margaret river
NERRIMA
HALL'S CREEK

PORT HEDLAND
Mt Goldsworthy
Barrow Island
WHIM CREEK
ROEBOURNE
MARBLE BAR
North West Cape
Robe river
NULLAGINE
Hamersley Range
WITTENOOM
Rough Range
RHODES RIDGE
Mt Tom Price
Mt Whaleback
Mt Newman

YINNIETHARRA
CARNARVON
THADUNA
Mt Gould
PEAK HILL
Murchison river
Weld Range
WILUNA
MEEKATHARRA

Tallering Peak
MT MAGNET
LAVERTON
NORTHAMPTON
LEONORA
GERALDTON
KOOLANOOKA
Mt Ida
YARDARINO
WATHEROO
KOOLYANOBBING
KALGOORLIE BOULDER
COOLGARDIE
KAMBALDA
SOUTHERN CROSS
PERTH
Darling Range
NORSEMAN
COLLIE
RAVENSTHORPE
BRIDGETOWN
ESPERANCE
AUGUSTA
Scott river
ALBANY

Oil
Iron
Asbestos
Silver
Coal
Mica
Salt
Alluvial Gold
Tin
Beryl
Nickel
Silica
Bauxite
Gold
Copper
Lead
Pyrite
Talc

Bureau of Mineral Resources, stated: *. . . there are hundreds of millions of tons of limonite-haematite-magnetite ore with a 20/30% metallic iron content . . . in the western half of the State southwards from Port Hedland.*

In 1960 the proved reserves of almost 500 million tons of iron ore were enough to supply foreseeable local needs for at least a century. The enormous but apparently poor-quality Pilbara reserves were available if they should ever be required. Unwanted and rarely mentioned, they were forgotten by the general public.

Not everyone forgot the northwest's iron country, particularly local prospectors living or working in the area. Several of these men, including Lang Hancock of Mulga Downs station near Mount Tom Price and Stan Hilditch of Meekatharra, became convinced that some of the "low grade" Pilbara iron reserves were in fact rich in high-quality ore. In 1952-3 Hancock discovered extensive deposits of limonitic ore in the Turner River area. Hilditch in 1957 found high-grade haematite ore in the Ophthalmia Range near Mount Whaleback. He later discovered most of the known important haematite reserves in the eastern Hamersley Range and the Ophthalmia Range.

R. G. Collins, a field engineer for the Broken Hill company, found limonite deposits along tributaries of the Ashburton River in 1958. B.H.P. geologists, J. E. Harms and B. D. Morgan, noted similar deposits from the air, along the Robe River valley. Another company employee, B. J. Vivian, sampled and mapped some of the Ashburton deposits in 1960. Later, in 1961, Harms and Morgan sampled the Robe deposits, using helicopters and Land Rovers.

When the Government lifted its embargo on the export of iron ore in 1960, Hancock, Hilditch and others took out extensive "temporary reserve" prospecting rights. Failing to interest Australian firms in their discoveries, the prospectors approached foreign mining companies. These organizations, faced with the loss of mining areas in emergent colonial countries round the world, had ready ears for the Australians.

Hancock allied himself with Conzinc Rio Tinto. This international mining firm later discovered high-grade haematite ore bodies on Hancock's leases around Mount Tom Price, and established the Hamersley Mining Company. Hilditch and his partner C. H. Warman, approached American Metal Climax. This company made a thorough geological survey of the partners' Mount Whaleback leases and became a major partner in the present-day firm of Mount Newman Mining Limited.

The Sentinel Mining Company of America obtained "temporary leases" of iron ore country round Mount Goldsworthy, 80 miles east of Port Hedland, and formed the Mount Goldsworthy Mining Company.

The B.H.P. Company took up "temporary reserves" of the Robe River area and later negotiated with the American firm of Cleveland Cliffs, Mitsui of Japan, and various Australian companies to begin mining.

Soon after the lifting of the iron ore export embargo in 1960, local and foreign

61

PILBARA MINERALS

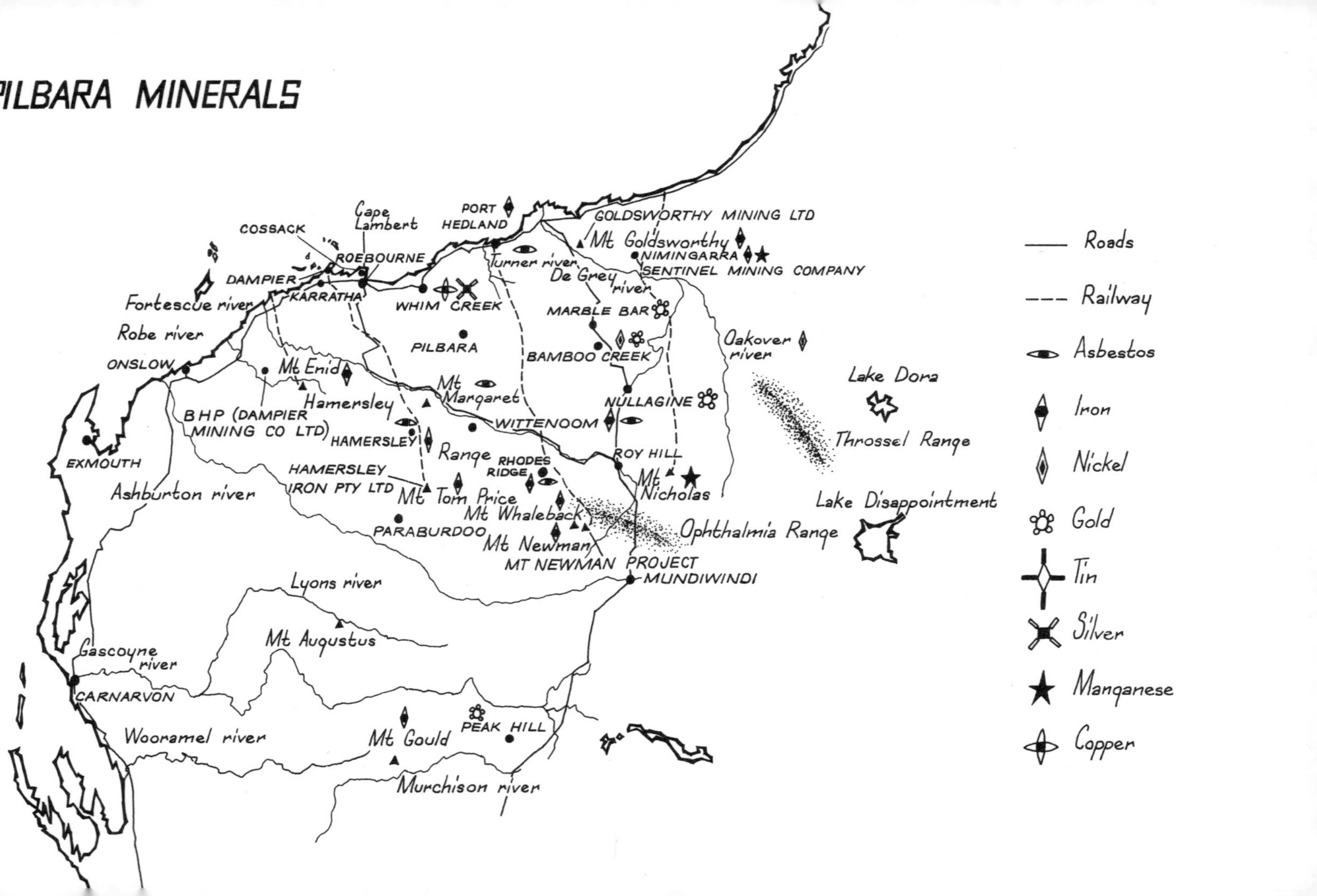

Legend:
- —— Roads
- --- Railway
- Asbestos
- Iron
- Nickel
- Gold
- Tin
- Silver
- Manganese
- Copper

Lake Dora

Throssel Range

Lake Disappointment

Oakover river

GOLDSWORTHY MINING LTD

SENTINEL MINING COMPANY

Mt Goldsworthy
NIMINGARRA

De Grey river

Turner river

MARBLE BAR

BAMBOO CREEK

NULLAGINE

Ophthalmia Range

ROY HILL

Mt Nicholas

MT NEWMAN PROJECT

MUNDIWINDI

PORT HEDLAND

WITTENOOM

Mt Margaret

RHODES RIDGE

Range

Mt Price

Mt Whaleback

Mt Newman

PEAK HILL

Murchison river

WHIM CREEK

PILBARA

HAMERSLEY

IRON PTY LTD

PARABURDOO

Mt Gould

Cape Lambert

ROEBOURNE

KARRATHA

Mt Enid

Hamersley

HAMERSLEY
(DAMPIER MINING CO LTD)

Lyons river

Mt Augustus

COSSACK

DAMPIER

BHP (DAMPIER MINING CO LTD)

Ashburton river

Fortescue river

Robe river

ONSLOW

Gascoyne river

CARNARVON

Wooramel river

EXMOUTH

prospectors had staked out millions of acres in the Pilbara and adjoining country. The stage was set for the New Frontier's great role as a mineral producer.

The new iron age

Iron is a silvery-white, tenacious, lustrous, malleable, ductile metal, rarely found native except in basalts and meteorites. It is magnetic, and can be magnetized, is brittle at very low temperatures, softens at red heat and can be welded at white heat. Pure iron has a specific gravity of about 7.9, a melting point of 1,530 degrees centigrade. Many minerals contain iron, which occurs throughout the earth's crust. There are enormous deposits on every major continent, including South America, North America, Africa, South-east Asia, China, Siberia, Russia, Europe — and Australia. The principal sources of the metal are the oxides haematite (70% iron), magnetite (72.4%), geothite (62.9%), limonite (up to 60%), and the carbonate siderite (48.3%). Steel is essentially iron alloyed with one or more elements such as carbon, manganese, silicon, chromium, or nickel. Iron is used on a far greater scale and over a far wider range of applications than any other metal.

Three years after the export embargo was lifted, proved iron ore deposits in the Pilbara district of Western Australia amounted to 15,000 million tons! A big jump from Australia's total proved iron ore reserves in 1960 of less than 500 million tons. These staggering discoveries were made largely on behalf of oversea mining firms already quarrying minerals in countries such as Africa, South America and South-east Asia.

The newly-discovered iron ore deposits in northwest Australia were not easy to sell on the over-supplied world market. After lengthy negotiations, the mining companies signed a series of long-term contracts with Japanese steel manufacturers, at prices somewhat below ruling world levels for iron ore. Most contracts covered the period 1966 to 1983, with some extending further.

It is interesting to note that Japanese steel-manufacturing firms do not bargain individually with oversea suppliers of raw materials. Instead they bargain collectively through a government convened consortium, which greatly increases their bargaining power on the over-supplied world iron ore market.

No major contracts were written with any other countries, though small amounts of iron ore were later exported to America and Europe. At July, 1970, more than 95% of all exported Australian iron ore was destined for Japan and further contracts being negotiated at that time were also with the Japanese. For the rest of this century, iron ore miners on the New Frontier will probably depend on Japan for a market — though Japan is not dependent on Australia for supplies. In the early 1970s, Japan bought about 30% of her iron ore requirements from Australia. This percentage was expected to rise to about 50% by the late 70s. Japan's other suppliers are Brazil, Chile, India,

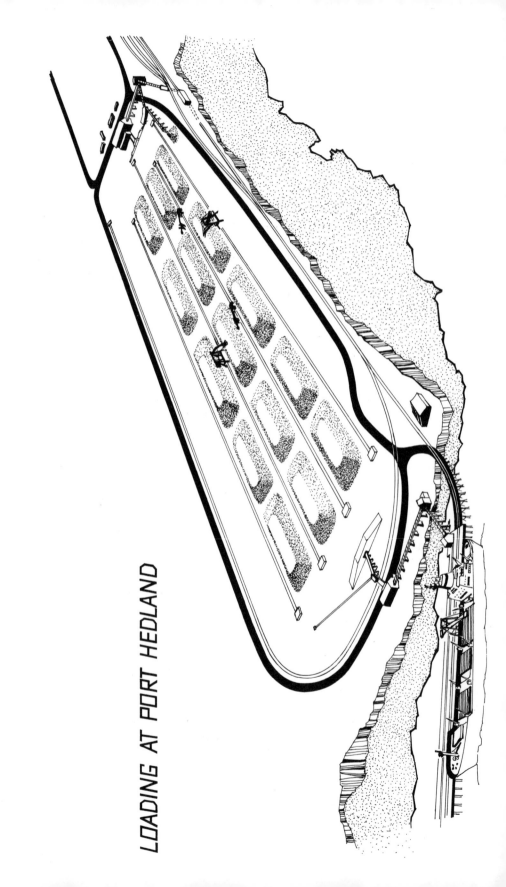

LOADING AT PORT HEDLAND

South Africa and various South-east Asian countries. Japan has also negotiated with China and the Soviet Union for iron ore supplies.

Although prices obtained for Australian iron ore were in some cases below those received by other countries, mining on the New Frontier has proved extremely profitable for the companies involved. These companies pay an average of less than 50 cents a ton (by way of royalty) for the ore which they sell at more than $9 a ton. Cost of production (mining, crushing transport) is up to $4 a ton – giving a profit of $4.50 a ton.

The true profitability of iron ore mining in northwest Australia is often misunderstood – perhaps because of the regular publication in the press of mining company profits "after tax". In the less widely read financial papers and mining journals, such as the *Australian Financial Review* and *The Australian Miner*, it is regularly acknowledged that special tax exemptions and deferments allow mining companies to escape taxation until the 1980s. (Even then, oversea investors will not pay Australian income-tax on dividends declared by the companies.)

If they were paying tax on their profits, companies might forfeit 45 cents in every dollar. This amount is not paid, but is, nevertheless, set aside each year as a provision against "future tax" (to be used meanwhile as working capital). The usual profit figure quoted is $2 a ton "after tax"; the true figure is nearer $4.50.

In February, 1970, Hamersley Holdings Limited (miners at Mount Tom Price) announced a profit of $25.3 million from the sale of 13 million tons of ore – representing a per-ton profit of just under $2.

The year's profit figure of $25.3 million was after deduction of $21.3 million for "future tax". Since this tax will not be paid, the actual profit for the year was $46.6 million––a profit per-ton of $3.50.

The published net profit figure was after a further deduction of $15.8 million for "depreciation" of plant. But early in 1968, the High Court allowed mining companies to deduct all development costs (which includes the full cost of all machinery, railroads and other "plant") for tax purposes. A proportion of this allowance is taken into consideration as "deductible capital expenditure" by companies when assessing profit for the year. Therefore no figure for "depreciation" should appear in statements concerning a company's profitability. This anomaly was pointed out by the influential *Financial Review* (on 14th March, 1968) when it stated "Hamersley's depreciation is purely a book entry as the Taxation Commissioner has allowed full deductions of the capital expenditure as part of mining allowances". The paper estimated the company's real profit for 1969 at between $50 and $60 million.

In fact it was $46.6 million, plus the book entry "depreciation" of $15.8 million – giving Hamersley a total profit of $62.4 million for the year ending December, 1969. This is considerably more than the published figure of only $25.3 million––and represents a per-ton profit of more than $4.50.

Moving from the particular to the general: at the beginning of 1970, the five major established iron ore mining companies on the New Frontier held contracts to export a total of 750 million tons of ore, chiefly to Japan. Their combined profit on these sales will be approximately $3,350 million.

Western Australia's share of the proceeds, from the average royalty of 45 cents a ton, will be about $350 million. From this must be deducted the cost of public works servicing the mining areas, which for the period 1968 to 1972 were estimated at $35 million (including $22 million for sealing the North West Coastal highway). Other public works between 1972 and 1983 will certainly require a further $40 million, possibly more.

This will reduce Western Australia's final return from existing contracts at the beginning of 1970, to round $275 million. This amounts to only 40 cents a ton, for ore on which the mining companies make a profit of $4.50 a ton.

What else will Australians get out of the mining bonanza? Local shareholders in the only New Frontier mining company with an appreciable Australian interest, Mount Newman, could expect to share $200 million over the 15-year period — though one of the partners, B.H.P., is notoriously slow declaring dividends.

Total Australian receipts, via royalties and dividends to investors, from the sale of 750 million tons of ore, are not likely to exceed $500 million. This does not compare very favourably with the figure of at least $3,350 million to be shared by the oversea interests in the mining companies.

Australia may reap some additional benefits from the sale of 750 million tons of iron ore when the mining companies begin to pay income-tax. It appears unlikely that the mining companies will pay any appreciable taxation to the Federal government before 1980.

It is difficult to obtain information concerning the amount of taxation to be paid by the companies and when this will be paid, for both the mining companies and the Western Australian Government claim that this information is confidential.

A similar situation exists concerning royalties actually paid — the author wrote three letters in 1969 to Charles Court, Minister for Industrial Development and the North West, asking for information on how much had so far been paid in royalties by Pilbara mining companies. In his replies, Mr Court gave no figures nor promised any. The author eventually obtained the information on royalties, listed below, through a question asked in the Legislative Assembly on 17th March, 1970.

Total Pilbara royalties paid to the State Government of Western Australia to December 31, 1970:

Hamersley Holdings Limited: $13.074 million

Goldsworthy Mining Limited: $5.733 million

Mount Newman Iron Ore Co.: $1.003 million

Hamersley, the largest operator, had shipped a total of 28 million tons of ore to 31st December, 1969. They paid a royalty of only 46 cents a ton.

Apart from royalty payments, the State of Western Australia receives a variety of benefits from the New Frontier's mining boom, though these have been somewhat exaggerated. The number of permanent jobs created by the mining industry has not been great. Many of the construction workers and railroad gangs are only temporary residents of the Pilbara and Ashburton districts.

The town of Newman, for example, has a total population of less than 2,000; the population of Tom Price is about the same. Dampier has around 3,000 residents. Port Hedland's population has, at times, exceeded 6,000, but it fluctuates considerably, according to what construction projects are in progress. Before the mining boom, Port Hedland's population was round 2,000, but could reach 10,000 in the mid-1970s.

The early construction period of the northwest's iron ore mining projects gave a boost to a limited number of Australian industries supplying building materials and machinery, but most of the major contracts for mining equipment, railroads and port installations went to large oversea companies.

Further expansion projects are in progress, or in the planning stage, but the initial pioneering clamour in the northwest has abated. Already-established mining towns and ports are mostly static, with comparatively small populations and little prospect of further expansion and diversification.

Other towns and ports will be established, but they are unlikely to be larger or more populous than the existing centres. The number of new citizens in the Pilbara in 1970 (round 12,000) will probably not double before 1980. Overall population may then reach 30,000.

The Robe River Project began taking shape in 1970, and expected to export its first ore in 1972, with a rise to 10 million tons yearly by 1975 (six million tons of ore and four million tons of pellets). Major shareholders in the project were Mitsui of Japan, Cleveland Cliffs of America and a consortium of Australian interests including Garrick Agnew Proprietary Limited and Mineral Securities Australia Limited.

It was announced early in 1970 that Texas Gulf Sulphur Limited of America was negotiating with Hanwright Limited of Australia to develop the local prospecting company's temporary reserves at Rhodes Ridge and Bakers Ridge, 35 miles northwest of Newman township. Another ore deposit called McCamey's Monster, was mooted for development in the 70s.

Colourful and imaginative pictures have been painted of future northwest development — of great cities to arise, centred on large industrial complexes, in turn surrounded by wide green swathes of flourishing agricultural land.

This kind of growth did not take place at Mount Isa, Broken Hill or Kalgoorlie, and

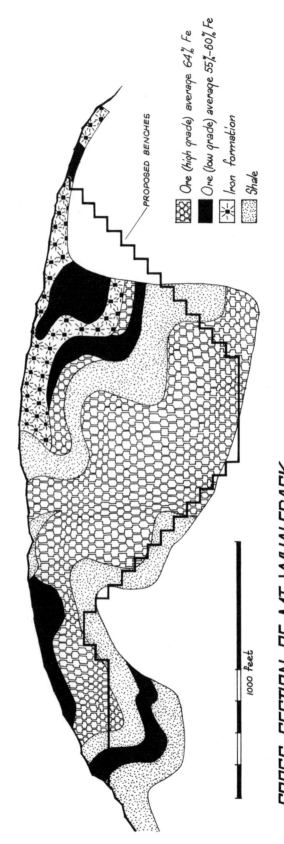

CROSS SECTION OF MT WHALEBACK

Ore (high grade) average 64% Fe

Ore (low grade) average 55%-60% Fe

Iron formation

Shale

PROPOSED BENCHES

1000 feet

it seems unlikely to occur round the New Frontier's mining towns — for similar reasons.

The mining towns and ports are set in arid, inhospitable areas of rock and spinifex, unsuited to agriculture, physically and climatically. The soil, what there is of it, is poor; rainfall is low and annual temperatures are among the highest in Australia. (The Pilbara mining area is closer to the equator than is Rockhampton, on the east coast, but receives only a fraction of the east coast's rainfall and is subject to hot, dry winds for much of the year.)

It has been suggested that steel-manufacturing will become an industry in the northwest. Some mining company agreements with the State of Western Australia call on the companies to set up secondary processing facilities for iron ore. This has been taken to mean steel-manufacture in some popular press stories, but in fact refers only to pelletizing of a small percentage of the companies' total output of iron ore. (Pelletizing is a method of increasing the iron content of the shipped ore. The Hamersley company's HImet pellets contain more than 90% iron, enabling them to be fed direct into electric steel-making furnaces, instead of first being processed by conventional blast furnaces into pig iron. The first HImet plant will be completed in 1973, at a cost of up to $100 million — reducing the company's future tax liability by a similar amount.')

In some contracts, the companies have until 1980 to establish pelletizing facilities and there are adequate escape clauses if by that time they consider it uneconomic to proceed (Clauses 12 and 13 in the Mount Goldsworthy Agreement and Clause 15 of the Amendment to the Hamersley Agreement, for example). There is therefore no real basis for the popular concept that mining companies are legally bound to establish steel-manufacture industries in northwest Australia.

In passing, it is interesting to note that in various contracts with the Western Australian Government inducements are high for the companies to begin pelletizing iron ore as soon as possible — such as reduced royalties, from 60 cents a ton of raw iron ore, down to 10 cents a ton if pelletizing commences before 1975 (after that, the rate rises from 15 cents to a maximum of 20 cents a ton of iron pellets).

Despite the inducements in their contracts, the companies, at the beginning of the 1970s were pelletizing only a small proportion of the iron ore mined. Hamersley, with one pellet plant at its port of Dampier (built in 1968), had studied the feasibility of a second plant in Japan, as an alternative to further expansion of pelletizing in Australia. The site of the proposed HImet plant had not been announced in March 1970.

Mining companies have shown little or no interest in the suggestion that they should begin steel-manufacturing in the northwest. This may be due to the fact that on the international market, steel is even harder to sell than iron ore. At present, the world's capability to produce steel exceeds demand by 80 million tons a year.

The New Frontier possesses only one of the many requirements for successful steel manufacture and sale — iron ore. The area lacks coal and a large resident work force, and is remote from potential steel-using customers. In their study of the world iron and steel industry, economists Hughes and Brown point out that all major steel producers are sited in heavy industrial areas, such as the Ruhr in Europe and Detroit and Chicago in America.

Hamersley Limited, the only potential steel-maker in northwest Australia, seemed to hold this view, when, in 1969-70, it took part in a joint study (with Armco Limited, America) of the Jervis Bay area on the east coast as a possible steel-making centre. This is close to the existing steel-making centre of Port Kembla and handy to all likely east coast steel buyers.

Overall, the prospect of northwest Australia's becoming a vast industrial complex based on steel manufacture is dim. Charles Court, Minister for Industrial Development and the North West, acknowledged in March, 1970, that the hoped-for Pilbara steel industry might not eventuate. He pointed out that the normally high cost of establishing steel-making facilities might be prohibitive in such a remote area. Also the large workforce required would need to be housed in new towns; and railways, roads and ports would have to be established. The additional cost of this "infrastructure" should not have to be borne by the mining and steel-making companies, Mr Court suggested. If they were relieved of this expenditure, a northwest steel industry might still be possible.

In view of Mr Court's suggestion that the State pay for the towns, railways, ports, roads and other facilities required by intending steel-manufacturing companies (such as Hamersley Mining Limited — annual profit $60 million) it is relevant to consider a previous example of government-financed infrastructure development. This is the Broken Hill Proprietary Limited's iron ore mine at Koolyanobbing and steel-making complex at Kwinana, south of Perth. The Koolyanobbing deposits of 100 million tons of ore were made available to B.H.P. on a royalty basis of round 25 cents a ton and the State of Western Australia undertook to build a 300-mile railway from the mine to Kwinana, for the transport of the ore, costing $100 million. As royalties will eventually total only $25 million, the cost of supplying this piece of infrastructure represents a loss to the State of $75 million! By 31st December, 1969 the Government's total royalties from Koolyanobbing ore were only $382,353.

Apart from these economic reasons, the arid climate and generally inhospitable geography of the Pilbara and adjacent ore mining centres present almost insurmountable barriers to large-scale general development and settlement.

The hinterland of the New Frontier between Geraldton and Port Hedland, despite the fabulous riches it has produced, seems destined for the same fate as similar country round Mount Isa, Broken Hill and Kalgoorlie. Over the harsh landscape of these long-established Eldorados there wander only a few sheep and cattle.

Development of the New Frontier's iron ore country will continue along established lines. New open-cut mines will be developed and these will be serviced by small company-owned towns designed to house the small workforce required for the highly

MT NEWMAN PROJECT

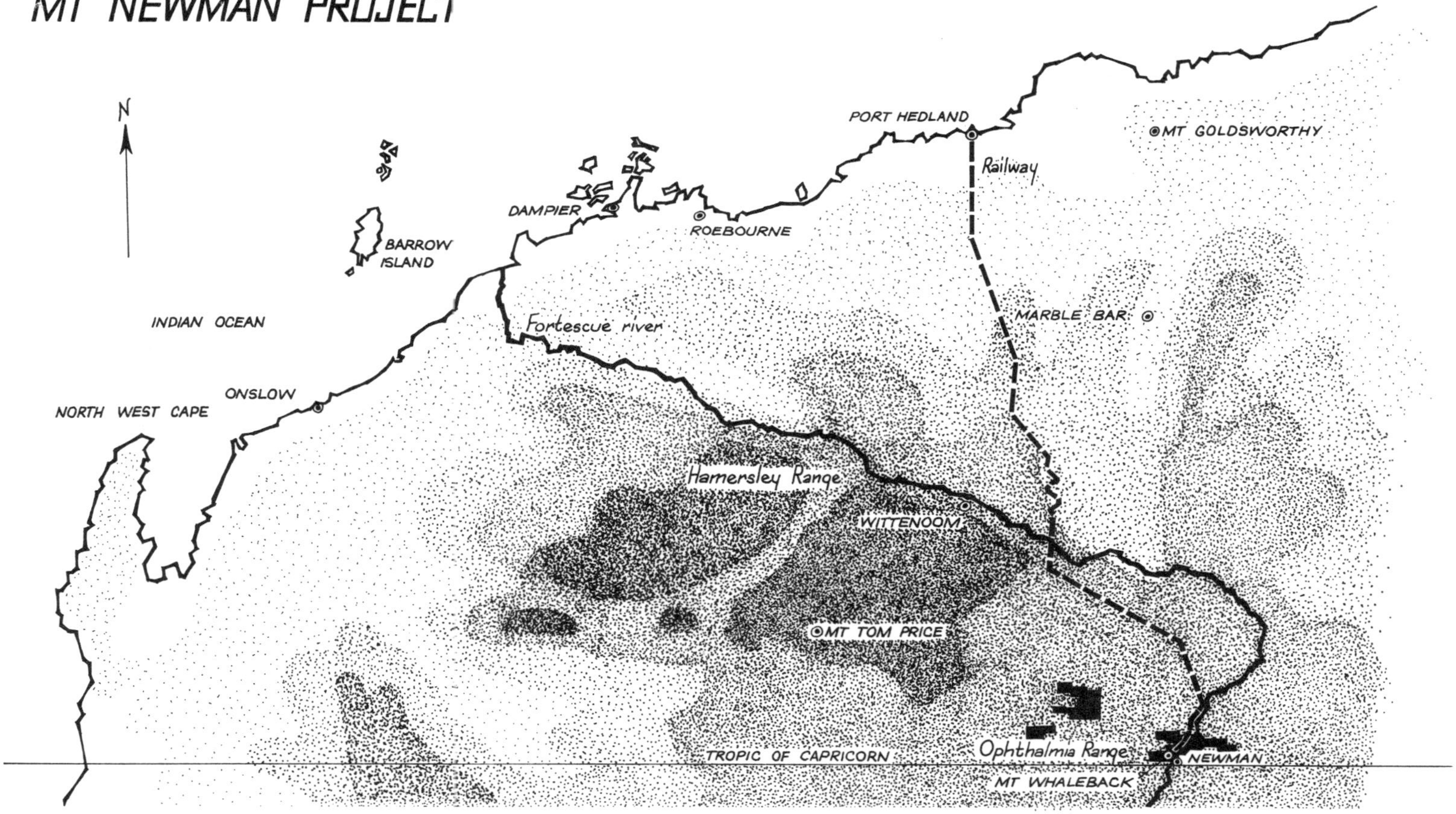

N

INDIAN OCEAN

NORTH WEST CAPE

ONSLOW

BARROW ISLAND

DAMPIER

ROEBOURNE

Fortescue river

Hamersley Range

WITTENOOM

MT. TOM PRICE

PORT HEDLAND

Railway

MARBLE BAR

MT GOLDSWORTHY

NEWMAN

Ophthalmia Range

MT. WHALEBACK

TROPIC OF CAPRICORN

mechanized operations. Of all the new settlements established in mining areas since 1966, Port Hedland was, in 1970, the only town not completely company-owned.

The concept of the company town is rather new to Australia. A company town is virtually private property, with everything on it and in it owned by the company concerned. This includes all housing, streets, parks, hotels, motels, shops, parking areas, caravan parks, camping areas, even post offices, schools and police stations (though these are staffed by government employees). The result of this is that no one can work, live or even stay temporarily in a company town unless the company so wishes. Anyone the company does not want in its town can be asked to leave. A person failing to comply with a request to leave can be evicted as a trespasser — by police action, if necessary. The situation arose in Mount Isa, Queensland, in the mid-1960s, when union representative Pat Mackie was barred from the town. Gamblers, thieves, prostitutes, and other undesirables — even union organizers — can be summarily evicted from a company-owned town.

Trains, lines, rolling stock, telephone systems and buses all belong to the company. The public may use the roads and railways provided this does not interfere with the company's activities (and provided intending passengers bring their own railway carriages, as there are no passenger cars on the giant ore trains). Telephones can be installed only through a request by the company and not simply on application by residents of the town.

Company-owned towns such as those in the mining areas of the New Frontier, have been criticized as contrary to democratic freedom — "alien blemishes in the national fabric of democratic living".

Despite blemishes and criticisms, the expansion of the mining industry by oversea companies on the New Frontier has been spectacular. World-wide publicity has been given to the unprecedented scale and speed of development amid the rock and spinifex of the Pilbara region. Towns, mines, railway lines and ports have mushroomed in the previously empty landscape — in some cases, such as the Hamersley project, the whole basic operation taking less than two years.

Newspapers, magazines, radio stations and television networks round the world have documented the sensational rush-to-riches on the mineral fields. Most of the publicity has high-lighted the physical immensity and impressive technology of the iron ore bonanza. Huge power-shovels, diesel trains and ore ships have fascinated the news cameras; impressive statistics have blazed in the headlines; public relations hand-outs from the mining companies and the puffings of politicians have featured on countless front pages.

Thoughtful, analytical appraisals of the mining "boom" have been few in the popular press. What did the New Frontier's mineral boom amount to, from the Australian point of view, at the beginning of the 1970s? Four major companies were mining ore in the Pilbara region — the Goldsworthy Mining Company (American owned), the Western Mining Company (American owned), Hamersley Mining

72

Company Limited (American owned), and Mount Newman Mining Company Limited (American, British, Japanese and Australian owned). Other American, Canadian, British and Japanese interests were negotiating to establish further mining and export facilities — United States Steel, the world's biggest steel producer, Texas Gulf Sulphur and Cleveland Cliffs of America, and Mitsui of Japan. The Belgian company, Union Miniere SA, faced with the possible loss of its huge copper deposits in the trouble-spot, Katanga, in Africa, was another eager mineral searcher in northwest Australia.

In 1970, Hamersley commenced developing its new mine and town at Paraburdoo, a few miles southwest of Tom Price. To handle the Paraburdoo production, a new port and town was under construction at Karratha, 10 miles from Dampier. This was jointly financed by the Hamersley company and the Western Australian Government, and intended to be a "non-company" town — an example of government-backed infrastructure development. A 63-mile rail link between town and port was surveyed and total expenditure on the new development estimated at $250 million. Population of Paraburdoo was expected to be round 2,000, and that of Karratha somewhat larger.

The Australian prospecting firm of Hanwright negotiated with the Mount Newman Mining Company and Texas Gulf Sulphur to mine ore on its extensive temporary reserves near Wittenoom. The feasibility of using atomic blasts for mining came under investigation.

American, Japanese and Australian business interests prepared to mine and export ore at Mount Enid and to develop a new town at the Robe River mouth or Cape Lambert, near Cossack.

In the early 1970s, the combined production of the four mining companies was approximately 40 million tons of iron ore yearly. (By the mid-1970s, this is expected to double, with Hamersley producing close to 40 million tons yearly and Mount Newman "in excess of 30 million tons".)

To Australia as a nation, the mineral boom has meant about $20 million yearly by way of royalties — less the mounting cost of public works and "infrastructure". Some Australian manufacturing and construction firms have shared a small portion of the boom, which created up to 1970 a total of 5,000 new jobs for Australians. Only two Australian companies had a significant interest in mining activities and these were concentrated in a single organization. (A 30% Australian interest in the Robe River Project seemed likely but was not definite.) With the majority of the most promising prospecting areas held under lease by foreign mining organizations, local participation in future developments seems destined to diminish, rather than increase.

For most Australians the New Frontier's mining boom has been a loud bang.

Several Australian economists and financial writers have criticized the method of exploitation of the northwest's iron ore reserves, claiming that Australia's share in the returns from the sale of her iron ore deposits is far too low. Spokesmen for the oversea

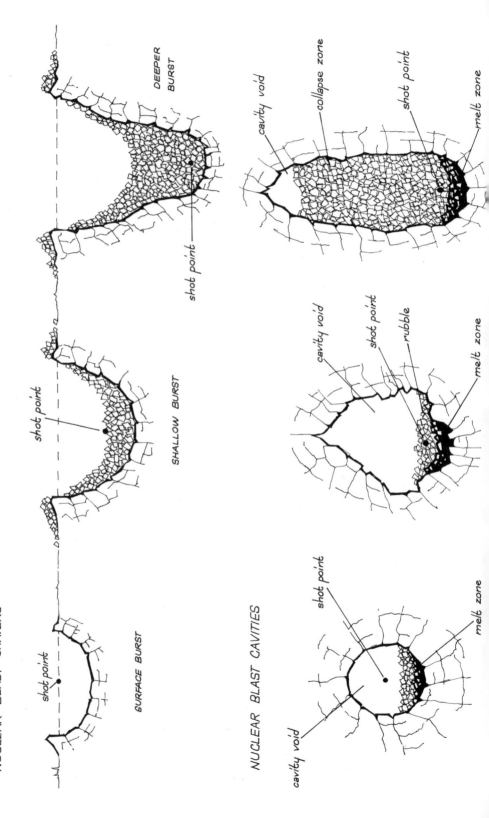

NUCLEAR BLAST CRATERS

shot point

SURFACE BURST

shot point

SHALLOW BURST

shot point

DEEPER BURST

NUCLEAR BLAST CAVITIES

shot point

cavity void

melt zone

cavity void

shot point

rubble

melt zone

cavity void

collapse zone

shot point

melt zone

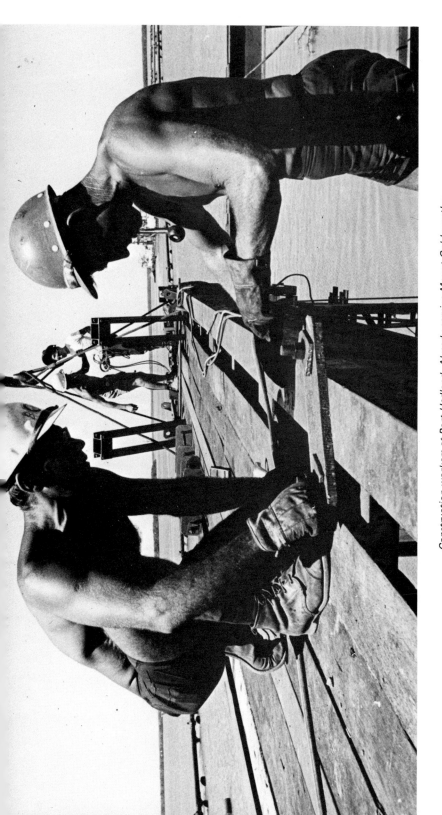

Construction workers at Port Hedland. Already serving Mount Goldsworthy and Mount Whaleback, the port may expand further to handle ore from new projects in the Hamersleys. Originally a sleepy fishing port of 2,000 inhabitants, Port Hedland may one day be an industrial community of 10,000 (W.A. government photo)

This sleepy inlet on Cape Lambert may be engulfed by a proposed iron port to serve the Robe River project

A British oil company uses this helicopter to fly workers to an offshore rig 60 miles out from Port Samson

General store at Broome established by a well-known northwest partnership in the pioneer days

Suburban development at Dampier, the iron port serving the Tom Price mine

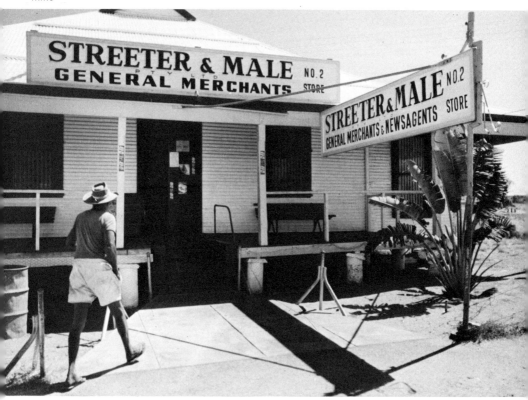

New buildings in Port Hedland are of modern tropical design

The old waterfront section of Port Hedland is typical of most Australian outback towns

The general store at Roebourne, the one-stop restocking centre for all travellers. Only beer and petrol need to be bought elsewhere in town

Sunset at the waterfront beer garden in Dampier

A Japanese ore carrier loading at a Pilbara iron port. Most ore (95%+) goes to Japan (W.A. government photo)

Aerial view of Broome, showing the deep-water jetty in the foreground. A few pearling luggers still operate from the old port and there is a small meatworks — but the town's future seems tied to tourism

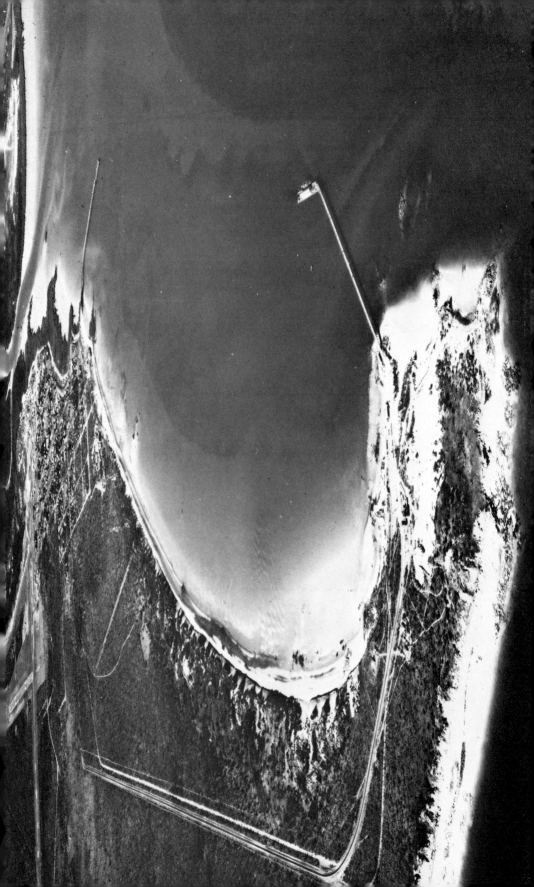

Late night mobile snack bar, Port Hedland

Old style shops in Port Hedland still flourish

mining companies have rejoined that Australian organizations either did not have the capital or were not prepared to risk it in iron ore mining.

What is the situation?

Some important basic facts concerning the development of the New Frontier's iron reserves are often overlooked.

Australian companies did not have sufficient available capital to develop the Pilbara ore reserves on the scale at which they have subsequently been exploited. Neither did the oversea companies now dominating Australian iron ore mining. In most cases these companies borrowed more than half the capital for their projects. Little, if any, financial risk was involved, apart from prospecting and ore-proving costs. Mining of the ore bodies and the construction of railways and ports did not begin until contracts were finalized. Money was then borrowed on the security of contracts with Japan to supply ore for 10- and 15-year periods.

Was there an alternative to the present largely foreign exploitation of the northwest's iron ore reserves? Critics of the existing situation suggest that an organization like that of the Snowy Mountains Authority, backed by the Australian Federal Government, could have efficiently developed the Pilbara ore deposits. Such an organization could have proved the deposits, negotiated the contracts and borrowed money on the international money-market, just as readily as the foreign mining companies. (Brazil followed this practice, and their state-owned Rio Doce and CVRD mines now export more than 20 million tons of iron ore yearly——for which a higher price is obtained than is paid for Australian ore.)

In January, 1970, the Australian Federal Government belatedly announced plans to form an Industrial Development Corporation to finance and develop the nation's mineral resources. In March, Prime Minister John Gorton told the Australian Mining Industry Council that he wanted to see greater Australian ownership in mineral development. The proposed Industrial Development Corporation would enable Australia to compete in oversea borrowings with the giant international companies.

Unfortunately, private companies already control sufficient iron ore reserves to supply world markets for at least half a century. The situation is similar with nickel, lead and bauxite – oversea companies control sufficient deposits to supply all foreseeable markets for many years to come.

Suggestions for an Industrial Development Corporation were made in the late 1950s, to retain the identity and skills of the Snowy Mountains Authority's complex of planners and technicians. Unfortunately, nothing was done for more than a decade.

The proposed Industrial Development Corporation seems destined to be confronted by the immense, nation-wide *fait accompli* of the largely-foreign mining companies.

Early proposals for Australia to develop its own iron ore and other mineral deposits were met with the claim that Australia had neither the capital nor the technical know-how to do the job. A Federal government-backed organization such as the proposed Industrial Development Corporation could have borrowed money just as readily as individual mining companies, who have borrowed sums up to $150 million.

The charge that Australian technology was not equal to the task of establishing open-cut mines, railways and ports cannot be sustained. Victoria's long established, open-cut brown coal mine at Yallourn, the Broken Hill Company's nation-wide ore-mining and steel-making complex and the Snowy Mountains Scheme all testify to the ability of Australians to conceive, develop and operate large-scale mining and engineering ventures. Open-cut iron ore mining, rail-roading and bulk-loading onto ships is a relatively simple engineering operation, as industrially "backward" Brazil has shown.

Further large mineral finds will almost certainly be made throughout Western Australia. Ownership of these minerals is vested in the Crown, which represents the Australian people. It is hoped that through an organization such as the Australian Industrial Development Corporation, a greater proportion of the profits of future mining bonanzas will stay in Australia, instead of being exported, together with the minerals.

Nickel – and the Poseidon "rush"

While the Pilbara iron miners were digging-in ready for production, prospector's drills probed for other riches beneath the inhospitable surface of the New Frontier. The search took place 600 miles southeast of the Hamersley Ranges, not far from the ailing gold mining town of Kalgoorlie and already defunct Coolgardie.

The goal of this hunt was one of the world's most valuable minerals: nickel, worth about $2,500 a ton. (In periods of scarcity, it has been worth around $10,000.) Its presence in Australia was unknown until 1947, when a farmer and a prospector picked up samples near Lake Lefroy, about 35 miles southeast of Kalgoorlie and close to the long-abandoned Red Hill gold-mine.

The two men, George Cowcill and John Morgan, revealed the site of their find to the American Western Mining Corporation, in 1964. After drilling, the Corporation announced big nickel deposits in 1966 at Kambalda, beside Lake Lefroy. Value of the reserves now stands at $1,500 million. The two prospectors were given a reward by the Corporation of $25,000 each.

In the initial stages, the Kambalda mine produced 5,000 tons of nickel yearly. By the mid-1970s, output will rise to 30,000 tons, worth more than $75 million. Royalty paid to the Western Australian Government is 2% of the value of the nickel extracted. This amounts to about $1.5 million annually for the people of the State, while the company grosses $75 million, less its mining and refining costs.

Nickel is used in the manufacture of tough, light, heat-resistant steel alloys. World demand has increased greatly since the general introduction of jet aircraft engines and the large-scale manufacture of rocket missiles. Nickel alloys are also used extensively in space rocket construction.

Following the Western Mining Corporation's successful Lake Lefroy venture, scores of other prospectors began searching for nickel in the area. Late in 1969, two mining companies in partnership, Great Boulder Gold Mines Limited and North Kalgurli (1912) Limited, announced two major nickel finds between 35 and 60 miles northeast of Kalgoorlie. Initial estimates put the total value of the deposits at $120 million.

In January, 1970, Western Mining located more nickel at Mount Clifford, 35 miles northwest of Leonora. Another explorer, Bowlake Nickel and Gold Pty Ltd, announced a nickel find at Bamboo Creek, near the Oakover River, inland from Marble Bar. (In the same month, Cominco of Canada and an Australian company both announced uranium strikes at near-by Nullagine.)

In 1969, a nickel prospecting company called Poseidon explored the Laverton area, about 200 miles northeast of Kalgoorlie. The market value of its 20 cent shares at the time was around 5 cents.

Late in 1969 rumours began circulating, first in the prospecting district and later on the stockmarket, that Poseidon had discovered large nickel deposits. The value of the company's shares began to increase, steadily at first, then rapidly in a phenomenal value explosion, to a crescendo of clamorous buying that echoed round the world's stock markets.

Shares that had sold at 5 cents in August, 1969, rocketed to $55 in November. By January, 1970, the shares were changing hands at a staggering $210 each!

By that time, the company's drilling tests had proved four million tons of nickel ore, giving the shares an ore-backed value of only $127 each. But informed estimates indicated that a total of at least 10 million tons of ore would eventually be proved by drilling. This would give Poseidon shares an ore-backed value of $317 each.

Poseidon's success encouraged a frenzy of nickel prospecting over thousands of square miles of adjacent country. What new discoveries will be made and the ultimate true value of Poseidon's strikes remains to be seen. (By mid-1970, Poseidon shares were down to $70.) At the beginning of the 1970s, only the Western Mining Corporation at Kambalda was actually mining nickel ore. Its output was approximately 6% of world production. The crushed concentrates are treated at the company's $50 million nickel refinery at Kwinana, south of Fremantle.

Early in 1970, some nickel prospectors had begun to concentrate on the Oakover River country, on the edge of the Great Sandy Desert. Whether or not this area will produce another Aladdin's Cave of mineral treasures remains an unanswered question.

Copper — at Whim Creek, the Mount Isa rival

Huge reserves of copper ore, totalling round 36 million tons, have recently been proved at Whim Creek, a derelict mining village half-way between Port Hedland and Roebourne. Japanese interests spent $1 million prospecting the area, but abandoned their search.

The lease was taken up by Canadian-American companies, under the name of Whim

Creek Consolidated Limited. These prospectors located copper ore bodies that may lead to a mining development rivalling Mount Isa in Queensland. Another American organization, Texas Gulf, controls the remainder of the ore bodies not owned by Whim Creek Consolidated.

Apart from royalties received for the copper extracted, Australia seems destined to have no significant share in the developing Whim Creek copper bonanza.

Oil search — on and off shore

In the 1930s, the Freney Kimberley Oil Company drilled unsuccessfully for oil in the Fitzroy basin of the Kimberleys. There was another brief search round Exmouth Gulf in 1940.

In 1946, Sir Harold Raggatt, former permanent head of the Department of National Development, suggested that oil-searching companies should drill in the nothern Carnarvon Basin. This is in the Exmouth Gulf region, astride the Ashburton River.

American backed companies took up the search in this area in 1951. The main companies involved were Standard Oil of California, Shell and Texaco Incorporated. An Australian firm, Ampol, was a minor partner in the venture, which operated under the name of West Australian Petroleum Pty Ltd. This organization became known as Wapet and though it is popularly allied with the name of Ampol, the relatively tiny Australian partner holds only a one-seventh share in Wapet. One third of the shares in Ampol are in the hands of the Australian public, so local interest in the Wapet organization is small.

The first oil strike in Australia was made on 5th September, 1953, at Rough Range, but unfortunately the find was not economical.

In May, 1964, after drilling more than 90 holes at a total cost of $40 million, Wapet discovered gas at Yardarino. A month later it struck oil on Barrow Island, about 40 miles off shore between Onslow and Roebourne. After follow-up drilling, Barrow Island was declared a commercial oilfield in May, 1966. Total cost of the find was $70 million.

Early in 1970, Barrow Island was producing around 35,000 barrels of oil daily. This was scheduled to increase to 45,000 barrels in 1971. Total reserves of recoverable oil are estimated at 114 million barrels, worth over $330 million. Studies are being made of methods to recover further reserves of oil known to exist, but which are not at present economically accessible.

The first shipment of crude oil left Barrow Island in April 1967. Since then, hundreds of additional wells have been drilled to boost production to its present level.

Encouraged by its success on Barrow Island, the Wapet consortium is now spending around $26 million yearly on further oil searches. An off shore drilling programme commenced in 1967 when the jack-up drilling rig *Jubilee* was towed 14,000 miles from Port Arthur, in Texas, to drill off the Western Australian coast.

Other companies have joined the search for oil on the New Frontier. In 1970, a

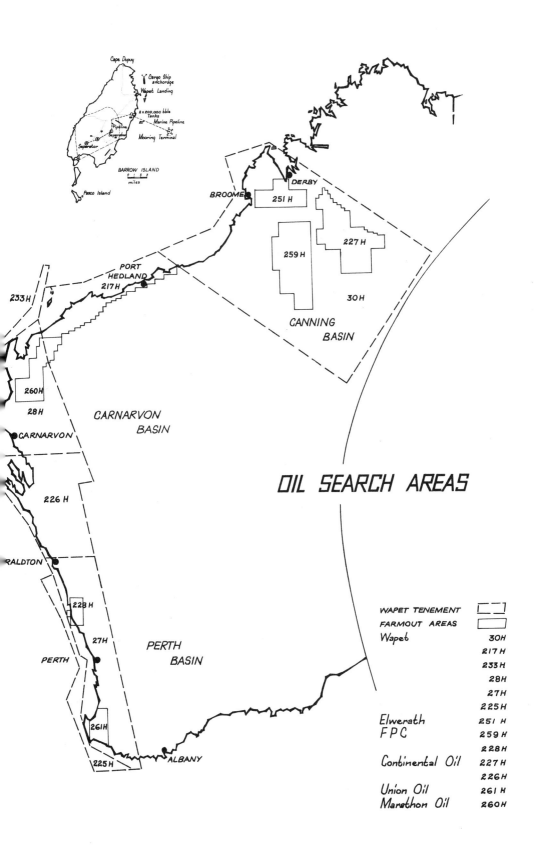

Cape Dupuy

Cargo Ship anchorage

Wapet Landing

2 x 200,000 bbls Tanks

Pipeline
Separator
20" Marine Pipeline

Mooring Terminal

Separator

BARROW ISLAND

miles

Pesco Island

DERBY

BROOME

251 H

259 H

227 H

30 H

CANNING

BASIN

PORT
HEDLAND

217 H

233 H

260 H

28 H

CARNARVON

BASIN

CARNARVON

226 H

RALDTON

228 H

27 H

PERTH
BASIN

PERTH

261 H

225 H

ALBANY

OIL SEARCH AREAS

WAPET TENEMENT	
FARMOUT AREAS	
Wapet	30H
	217 H
	233 H
	28 H
	27 H
	225 H
Elwerath	251 H
FPC	259 H
	228 H
Continental Oil	227 H
	226 H
Union Oil	261 H
Marathon Oil	260 H

dozen foreign oil explorers were active in and near Western Australia. The British giant, Burmah Oil Company, concentrated its efforts 70 miles out to sea off Port Samson, near Cossack. Another oversea driller, Arco Limited, stationed a $10 million Japanese drilling rig in the Bonaparte Gulf, near Wyndham. Other big explorers included French Petroleum, Continental Oil and Union Oil.

To date, Wapet has been the most successful, locating more oil on Pasco Island, not far from Barrow Island. Natural gas in commercial quantities has been discovered at Dongara.

Predictions cannot be made of further oil strikes on the New Frontier. Judging from the number of prospectors engaged in drilling, and the scope of their activities, it seems probable that if more oil is present in Western Australia or adjacent waters, it will be discovered by the oversea companies now searching for it.

Travel

The New Frontier has become the land of the guided tour, and of air travel. There are plenty of places and things to see — though widely spaced and separated by enormous expanses of monotonous, nondescript country, of interest only to the naturalist or fossicker.

Major roads are chiefly of earth construction, often badly corrugated, pot-holed, sandy or muddy. The only major length of sealed bitumen road, the coastal route from Perth to Port Hedland, is scheduled for completion in the mid-1970s. Minor roads, usually no more than tracks, often require four-wheel drive vehicles. Sign-posting is poor, even on major routes, and elsewhere non-existent.

A considerable number of motorists tour the west each year, some of them towing caravans — but few do the trip a second time, or recommend it to others.

Apart from the rough roads and tremendous distances, accommodation presents a problem for the itinerant motorist. Each town usually has only one hotel or motel, almost invariably permanently booked out. There is no room for the casual arrival. To obtain accommodation, you must book weeks or months in advance and limit your touring holiday to a strict schedule of arrivals and departures, quite out of keeping with the concept of a carefree motoring safari. Bad roads, floods and break-downs make it extremely difficult to adhere to timetables in the northwest. Break-downs, even minor ones, cause long roadside delays, because garages are often hundreds of miles apart.

Motel accommodation when it is available on the New Frontier is expensive. An overnight stay with breakfast for two people costs between $20 and $25! This is the ruling price in places such as Kununurra, Wyndham, Derby, Broome, Port Hedland, Dampier and Tom Price.

Provided time isn't important, caravan touring in the northwest can be enjoyable. Three months is a realistic minimum period. The van should not be large and needs to be exceptionally rugged to withstand thousands of miles of extremely rough, corrugated roads. Conventional cars are often used as towing vehicles, but four-wheel drive units are more suited to the job.

The distances involved in a car tour óf the New Frontier are considerable, even by Australian standards. From the east coast, it is roughly 3,000 road miles to Geraldton, on the southern limit of the New Frontier. Travelling across the top of Australia, the distance to Kununurra on the Ord River Project is about the same — 3,000 miles. Such a journey by car and caravan takes at least two weeks, preferably longer. This means a total of a month or six weeks, just getting to and from the New Frontier by car.

Allowing for a few sight-seeing detours on the way, the road distance between Kununurra and Geraldton is round 2,000 miles. Thus a motoring tour of only the sketchiest profile of the New Frontier adds up to 8,000 miles. Many who do the trip record 10,000 miles. With these driving distances and the state of the roads, a motoring tour of northwest Australia should not be undertaken lightly.

Inadequately sign-posted roads and the large number of as yet unmapped roads and tracks under construction, often make it hard to find your way in a vehicle. This can be time-consuming, annoying, even dangerous in lonely areas. Enough surplus water and food for a week should be held in reserve, in case of emergencies. The motorist should also carry adequate tools and spare parts for the more common forms of break-down.

Conducted tours, if you can afford them, are the best way to explore the New Frontier, and plane travel compresses otherwise monotonous journeys. Coastal steamers cater for tourists and provide another form of travel worth investigating. Capital-city tourist bureaus can supply details of sea, air and bus tours.

A major advantage of the conducted tour is that visitors see more places of interest than they are likely to locate if left to their own devices. Many scenic attractions aren't mapped.

New points of interest are being discovered all the time, as mineral prospectors and miners carve tracks into previously inaccessible country. Drilling rigs, aboriginal cave paintings, rare wildlife, a hidden oasis or a fascinating geological formation may be only a few miles off the main road. The unguided visitor misses these points of interest because they are not sign-posted.

On the other hand, he will often search in vain for a scenic attraction marked on his map, unaware that the route has been changed — or be confounded by the inaccuracy of his printed guide, the proliferation of newly-made tracks, and the absence of sign-posts. Often, the mining camp or oil rig he is seeking has been moved since the tourist's guide-map was printed.

Major scenic attractions are few and far between on the New Frontier. There is no rival to Ayers Rock or Mount Olga, so the minor places of interest off the beaten track have considerable importance for the traveller setting out on the Great Northern Highway from Meekatharra for example, bound for the next large town. (From Meekatharra this is Port Hedland, about 600 dusty miles northward!) Without guidance on where to look for points of interest along the way and scenic detours, this can be a tedious, monotonous journey.

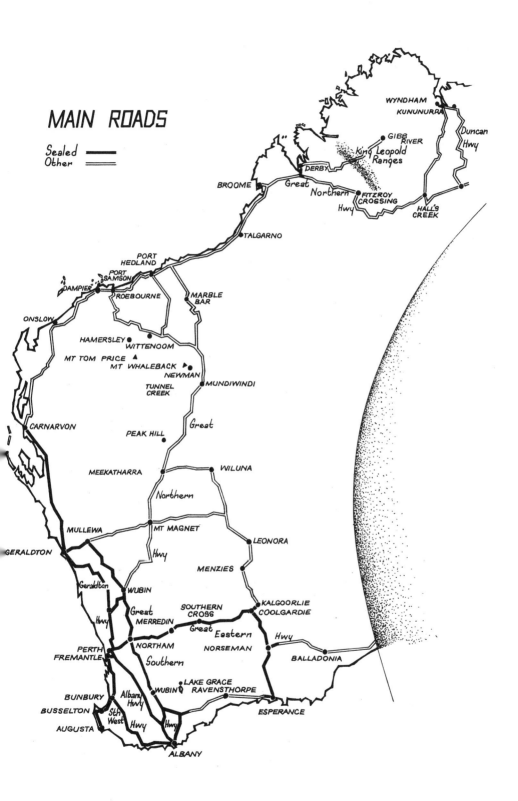

Tour buses on the Great Northern Highway iron out the bumps, keep out the dust, and detour to points of interest — such as the mining ghost town of Peak Hill and bustling, booming Newman, near the gigantic iron ore deposits under Mount Whaleback.

On organised tours, accommodation is arranged, at the only Motel at Newman, the one at Tom Price, and the one at Dampier; and at one of several modern motels at Port Hedland. The casual tourist arriving unannounced has Buckley's chance of landing motel accommodation at such towns. (There are a couple of water-front hotels and various boarding houses in Port Hedland, but they, like the motels, are usually booked out).

Air tours from Perth make it possible to visit all the major centres in the northwest in a single week. This is the most comfortable, the most convenient, and the most expensive way to see the New Frontier. For those with limited time, but the necessary cash, it is the best way to see the northwest. This applies also to those with no particular interest in savouring the full-flavour of the New Frontier — those whose major purpose is to view the new developments and the more popular landmarks, then scurry back to the air-conditioned comfort of their home city.

From Perth, an air tour of the Hamersley area takes three days, with visits to Tom Price, Wittenoom, Roebourne, Dampier, Point Samson and Port Hedland. A three-day tour of the Gascoyne district takes in Geraldton, Carnarvon, and Exmouth Gulf. A six-day Kimberley tour visits Kununurra, Wyndham and Ivanhoe stations, Derby, Fitzroy Crossing and Broome (with brief touch-downs at Port Hedland and other regular landing places between Perth and the Kimberleys).

A nine-day tour, Perth-Darwin-Perth, including all overnight accommodation, meals and also a total 400-miles of bus tours costs $500 (price in 1970). Tourists travelling one way only on this trip — Darwin to Perth, or Perth to Darwin — pay $300. By comparison a three-day tour of the Gascoyne district from Perth costs $150.

Short bus trips of a few hours' duration are included in the northwest air tours. These take in visits to the Ord Scheme, Geikie Gorge near Fitzroy Crossing, the town and port installations of Port Hedland, the Tom Price mine and Wittenoom Gorge. Overnight motel and hotel accommodation is part of these package deals.

For those with the inclination and time to visit the New Frontier "in depth", a camping or caravan tour is the best way. Only hardy types used to camping and rough, dusty living, should attempt this. Vehicles and all equipment must be sturdy and in first-class order. Equally important, those taking part in the expedition should know clearly that their journey will be arduous some of the time and dusty all of the time. It is unwise to plan a strict itinerary — an inch or so of rain on some major northwest roads can stop most traffic for several days.

More important, the motor tourist should be prepared to make unscheduled detours to places of interest as he discovers them. An adventurous, inquiring frame of mind is the major requirement for a successful tour of the New Frontier. Local information, gleaned at shops and pubs, can turn up more places of interest than many tourist pamphlets.

The ideal time for motor touring in the west is May to September — from October the weather is uncomfortably hot by southern standards. It is worth remembering that most of the New Frontier is north of the Tropic of Capricorn, which passes near Rockhampton on the east coast. The Kimberley area is in the same latitude as Cairns on the eastern side of the continent. Heavy rain may fall in December, as a prelude to the summer wet season, when most roads become impassable for long periods.

The town of Derby runs its annual Boab Festival during the first 10 days of August. Apart from the usual sporting events and street parades, the festival features a rodeo and an aboriginal corroboree. Touring motorists should make every effort to be in Derby for the first week in August and the Boab Festival.

A new road from Derby now provides access to the rugged, colourful Leopold Ranges. There are as yet no towns or road houses in the area, but the self-sufficient camper or caravaner should allow a three or four-day detour into this newly-opened country. The road is wide and well maintained, for cattle trains, and is ideal for caravans.

The section of road still under construction will eventually reach Gibb River, 300 miles from Derby. Cost of construction will be more than $600,000, a large sum to provide access to the small, lonely homestead at Gibb River. Local opinion is that the road will be continued farther to Port Warrender on the Admiralty Gulf. This is the site of the proposed huge bauxite mining project to be established by the American Metal Climax Corporation. This company has discovered enormous deposits of bauxite on its leases covering the Mitchell Plateau and other areas. At present there is no land access to the project site — and the true purpose of the magnificent and expensive "beef road" to Gibb River is therefore open to conjecture.

Meanwhile, it is without doubt an excellent tourist road, providing easy access to hitherto inaccessible areas beyond the King Leopold Ranges.

A bush track from the King Leopold beef road goes via scenic Winjana Gorge and Tunnel Creek to rejoin the highway a few miles west of Fitzroy Crossing. Some tour buses follow this route, but motorists should make careful inquiries in Derby before attempting it. Beyond Winjana Gorge the track is definitely not suitable for caravans, because of many steep creek crossings. Conventional vehicles can also find the going difficult, in creek crossings and on stony ridges where the track is extremely rough and ill-defined.

As a general rule, touring motorists should not venture off main roads unless they have recent, accurate, local information. This applies particularly to caravaners and motorists with limited experience of bush driving. Interesting side-roads on State and district maps have a habit of degenerating into narrow sand traps. Turning round to retrace your steps can be a difficult operation for a car, and impossible for a caravan. Spinifex, scrub, sand or boulders frequently hem in the traveller on what becomes a one-way track to nowhere.

In 1969, a motorist exploring a side track from the Great Northern Highway near Marble Bar got bogged in a dry sandy tributary of the De Grey River. He died of heat exhaustion while trying to extricate his vehicle. Other travellers in the northwest, broken-down, bogged or lost, have died similarly.

Above all motoring tourists should be careful when exploring off the beaten track, unless they have recent and reliable information on road conditions. Motorists with an adventurous bent should travel in four-wheel drive vehicles on the New Frontier.

Index